The Wake of Deconstruction

THE BUCKNELL LECTURES IN LITERARY THEORY
General Editors: Michael Payne and Harold Schweizer

The lectures in this series explore some of the fundamental changes in literary studies that have occurred during the past thirty years in response to new work in feminism, Marxism, psychoanalysis, and deconstruction. They assess the impact of these changes and examine specific texts in the light of this new work. Each volume in the series includes a critical assessment of the lecturer's own publications, an interview, and a comprehensive bibliography.

The Wake of Deconstruction

Barbara Johnson

BLACKWELL
Oxford UK & Cambridge USA

First published 1994
Reprinted 1995

Blackwell Publishers, the publishing imprint of Basil Blackwell Inc.
238 Main Street
Cambridge, Massachusetts 02142, USA

Basil Blackwell Ltd
108 Cowley Road
Oxford OX4 1JF
UK

Library of Congress Cataloging-in-Publication Data

Johnson, Barbara, 1947–
    The wake of deconstruction / Barbara Johnson.
       p.   cm. — (The Bucknell lectures in literary theory ; 11)
    Includes bibliographical references and index.
    ISBN 0–631–19014–7. — ISBN 0–631–18963–7 (pbk.)
    1. Criticism.   2. Deconstruction.   I. Title.   II. Series.
    PN85. J52 1994   93-42050
    801′.95—dc20   CIP

British Library Cataloguing in Publication Data

A CIP catalogue record for this book is available from the British Library.

Typeset in 11/13pt Plantin by Pure Tech Corporation, Pondicherry, India

Printed in Great Britain by Hartnolls Ltd, Bodmin

This book is printed on acid-free paper

In memory of Nietzschie
1980–1992

Contents

Preface

Fundamental and far-reaching changes in literary studies, often compared to paradigmatic shifts in the sciences, have been taking place during the last thirty years. These changes have included enlarging the literary canon not only to include novels, poems, and plays by writers whose race, gender, or nationality had marginalized their work, but also to include texts by philosophers, psychoanalysts, historians, anthropologists, and social and religious thinkers, who previously were studied by critics merely as 'background.' The stance of the critic and student of literature is also now more in question than ever before. In 1951 it was possible for Cleanth Brooks to declare with confidence that the critic's job was to describe and evaluate literary objects, implying the relevance for criticism of the model of scientific objectivity, while leaving unasked questions concerning significant issues in scientific theory, such as complementarity, indeterminacy, and the use of metaphor. Now the possibility of value-free scepticism is itself in doubt as many feminist, Marxist, and psychoanalytic theorists have stressed the inescapability of ideology and the consequent obligation of teachers and students of literature to declare their political, axiological, and aesthetic positions in order to make those positions conscious and available for examination. Such expansion and deepening of literary studies has, for many critics, revitalized their field.

Those for whom the theoretical revolution has been regenerative would readily echo, and apply to criticism, Lacan's call to revitalize psychoanalysis: 'I consider it to be an urgent task to disengage from concepts that are being deadened by routine use the meaning that they regain both from a re-examination of their history and from a reflexion on their subjective foundations. That, no doubt, is the teacher's prime function.'

Many practising writers and teachers of literature, however, see recent developments in literary theory as dangerous and anti- humanistic. They would insist that displacement of the centrality of the word, claims for the 'death of the author,' emphasis upon gaps and incapacities in language, and indiscriminate opening of the canon threaten to marginalize literature itself. On this view the advance of theory is possible only because of literature's retreat in the face of aggressive moves by Marxism, feminism, deconstruction, and psychoanalysis. Furthermore, at a time of militant conservatism and the dominance of corporate values in America and Western Europe, literary theory threatens to diminish further the declining audience for literature and criticism. Theoretical books are difficult to read; they usually assume that their readers possess knowledge that few who have received a traditional literary education have; they often require massive reassessments of language, meaning, and the world; they seem to draw their life from suspect branches of other disciplines: professional philosophers usually avoid Derrida; psychoanalysts dismiss Freud as unscientific; Lacan was excommunicated even by the International Psycho-Analytical Association.

The volumes in this series record part of the attempt at Bucknell University to sustain conversation about changes in literary studies, the impact of those changes on literary art, and the significance of literary theory for the humanities and human sciences. A generous grant from the Andrew W. Mellon Foundation has made possible a five-year series of visiting lectureships by internationally known participants in the reshaping of literary studies. Each volume includes a comprehensive introduction to the published work of the lecturer, the Bucknell Lectures, an interview, and a comprehensive bibliography.

Introduction

I

In the introduction to her translation of Derrida's *Dissémination*, Barbara Johnson notes that Derrida's new reading of various ancient and modern philosophers announces 'a revolution in the very logic of meaning' (xiii). Her own work carries this revolution into questions of identity and difference, first in their literary forms and more recently in explicitly racial, sexual, and political contexts. The subtle moral force of Johnson's work, its love of the minute particulars of difference, and its relentless pursuit of difficulty, owes a political debt to the 1968 May revolution in France, which demanded, as she writes, a 'liberation of the signifier, the rebellion against idealist repressions, and the unleashing of the forces of difference and desire against the law and order of identity.'[1] Her two most influential books, *The Critical Difference* (1980) and *A World of Difference* (1987)[2] underscore, through the repetition of 'difference' in their titles, Johnson's desire to differ – that is, to subvert the law and order of identity. As she points out, 'Nothing could be more comforting to the established order than the requirement that everything be assigned a clear meaning or stand' (*WD*, 30–1). Some of Johnson's subversive interest seems to express itself in numerous word plays and puns, as for example in her essay titles

'Mallarmé as Mother,' 'Apostrophe, Animation, and Abortion,' 'Les Fleurs du mal armé,' 'Allegory's Trip-Tease,' and in the titles of her books, *The Critical Difference* and *A World of Difference*, where the playfulness of words, their alliterations and duplicities, their always poetical correspondences – even when they have political assignments – mark the fortuitous and subversive nature of signification.

The introductions to both books announce that the readings of texts will proceed by exposing and dismantling 'the illusion created by the workings of differences,' because difference presupposes identity, and identity is inevitably based on a repression of differences. The word 'individual' itself marks this repression in its negation of divisibility. Perhaps tragically, it is the very repression of difference within and the positing of unity and identity that allows the creation and function of binary differences.

Allowing for two motivating forces for that repression, Johnson asks: Is difference determined by 'the complexities of fact or out of the impulses of power?' Is it a matter of 'description or disagreement, information or censure'? (*CD*, x) Johnson's most explicit answer to these questions is offered in the penultimate chapter of *A World of Difference*, where, in an essay on Zora Neale Hurston, she points out that 'What Hurston rigorously shows is that questions of difference and identity are always a function of a specific interlocutionary situation – and the answers, matters of strategy rather than truth' (*WD*, 178). Similarly, in her essay on Melville's *Billy Budd*, 'The legal order which attempts to submit "brute force" to "forms, measured forms," can only eliminate violence by transforming violence into the final authority' (*CD*, 109).

In order to trace the authority of political violence to its smallest linguistic source and denominator, Johnson unmasks that violence in 'the warring forces of signification' itself (*CD*, 5). For even 'as tranquil a notion as metaphor' is inherently violent (*CD*, 6). However, when in *The Critical Difference* she follows her intimations of a war within words into such pacific concepts as 'the poetic,' 'cookery,' 'hair,' and 'syntax,' these intimations might appear – in light of the subsequent book – as somewhat overdramatized by the canonical and aesthetic contexts in which they are discussed. By her own admission, in her revealing, but at the same time only seemingly straightforward introduction to *A World of Difference*, her earlier book, *Critical Difference*, had masked that violence 'within the sameness of the white male Euro-American literary, philosophical, psychoanalytical, and critical canon' (*WD*, 2). Surely, the implication here is that the 'sameness' of this canon is fictional and constructed, otherwise one would be somewhat perplexed to find Johnson ascertaining a 'sameness' on such large grounds, when in the same book it was not granted to a hair.

While in *The Critical Difference* questions about difference and identity are thus posed in a largely canonical and aesthetic context, her essay on Hurston exemplifies what the introduction to *A World of Difference* announces as a 'transfer [of] the analysis of difference . . . out of the realm of linguistic universality or deconstructive allegory . . . into contexts in which difference is very much at issue in the "real world" ' (*WD*, 2). However, the very conclusion reached in her essay on Hurston reconfirms the impression that even in a wider, non-canonical, politicized context, her project is still (as the subtitle of the earlier book had announced) a 'rhetoric of reading,' a matter of interlocutionary situation and verbal strategy. It seems that 'linguistic universality' remains the privileged center of Johnson's deconstructive project. If her transfer of 'deconstructive allegory' were intended to respond to Christopher Norris's charge that Johnson's work 'might yet become a kind of negative theology, perpetually rehearsing – or allegorizing – its own critical difference,'[3] then the charge seems not to have been refuted in *A World of Difference*.

But perhaps it cannot be. This conclusion, at least, appears anticipated in the 'Opening Remarks' to *The Critical Difference*, where Johnson assigns such attempts to 'go beyond' as already mired in logocentric assumptions: 'a binary opposition between oneself and what one attempts to leave behind' (*CD*, xi). The introduction to *A World of Difference*, therefore, presents its ideological transfer in the most circumspect of terms, highlighting in an exemplary manner the difficulties both in committing deconstructive readings to political action and, conversely, of disentangling political action from precisely those linguistic patterns that structure it and which in turn invite deconstructive readings.

The concepts of identity and difference between linguistic universality and the 'real world' thus establish for Johnson only 'some semblance' which allows her both to affirm and to doubt 'a progression' from *The Critical Difference* to *A World of Difference*. 'Linguistic universality' and the 'allegories of deconstruction' remain throughout the sixteen chapters of *A World of Difference*, as well as throughout the seven chapters of *Critical Difference*, 'an integral part of action' – including the action of the transference from deconstructive allegories to the world itself. Indeed, that 'transference' – Johnson's choice of this Freudian term seems strategic – is as interminable as were Freud's attempts to separate past events from present accounts.

The differences between Johnson's earlier and later work appear to dissolve as well in the admission that the last essay of her most recent book was anticipated eight years earlier in her first book *Défigurations, du langage poétique* (*WD*, 5). Johnson's admission of 'some semblance of a progression . . . from white male long-standingly canonical authors to white or black female authors'

proves likewise a self-consciously sceptical moral pil-
grimage as those authors 'are rapidly being canonized
even as I write' (*WD*, 4). Like the differences between
the masculine and the feminine or between literature
and criticism or sexuality and textuality in *The Critical
Difference*, which merely offer themselves as initial lures
'with a promise of comprehension' (*CD*, x), the differences between linguistic universality and the 'real world'
serve only as the steps of a ladder that is later to be
discarded.

The 'real world' to which we turn in the pages of *A
World of Difference* thus always appears under erasure, in
quotation marks. It is always a written world, though no
less real for being so conceived. And while differences
are inscribed by the violence of figuration in larger than
linguistic, social, and political circumstances, even there
they still appear, as Johnson points out, only '*as if*' they
had 'referential validity' (*WD*, 2). Predictably, then, the
same deconstructive allegories apply, revealing that
the warring forces of signification encode a 'politics of
violence' (*WD*, 184) and that the political context is
'structured like, and by, the contours of figurative language' (*WD*, 6).

Conversely, the most apparently harmless figurative
language – that of poetry – inhabits and shapes political
realities. For if 'Poetry makes nothing happen,' as
Johnson admits, at the same time 'poetry makes *nothing*
happen.' In the first, unitalicized instance it is purpor-
tedly 'outside the political,' but in the second it is 'the
stuff of the political' (*WD*, 30). Johnson allows poetry
an aesthetic respite from the world 'if and only if one is
attempting to follow an imperative not to stop there'
(*WD*, 31). The imperative takes its authority from a
rejection of an aesthetic solipsism, a stopping by woods
on snowy evenings or upon Westminster bridges, because these inward forms of otherness permit an idealization and neutralization of an otherness that would

amount to a synthesis of what always remains, and should remain, an unbridgeable difference within.[4] The italicized '*nothing*' thus reverberates for Johnson with political duplicity, or indeed with Kant's *Zweckmässigkeit ohne Zweck*, a purposeless purposefulness assigned to the aesthetic which has been accused of a reactionary complicity with the always deplorable status quo.

The privileges of such poetic ambiguity and undecidability might appear arch-conservative. But 'conservative,' in Johnson's work, has, predictably, a different meaning. When Johnson asks in one of her chapter titles, 'Is Writerliness Conservative?', the question remains undecidable because the word 'conservative' itself acquires radicality and a bit of ambiguity: 'writerliness itself is conservative only in the sense that it is capable of inscribing and conserving messages the radicality of which may not yet have been explored' (*WD*, 31). But the 'not yet . . . explored' promises itself a semblance of a progress; if it is to avoid the lure of comprehension, 'not yet' ought perhaps to mean never. If the writerly text conserves its secrets forever, it is not because it 'lies beyond the limits of knowledge, some unreachable, sacred, ineffable point toward which we vainly yearn' (*CD*, xii), but because 'cognition itself becomes an act of violence' (*CD*, 106); and in its very fever to quantify, 'knowledge becomes the obstacle to knowing' (*WD*, 85). The inscriptions and conservations of *le scriptible* remain thus like that fugitive hint of a story in Poe's tale 'The Purloined Letter,' always in sufferance. If these infinite impracticalities of writerliness seem equally (ir)relevant, as Johnson notes, 'not only to the left, but also to the right' (*WD*, 30), the sure and certain positioning of the Left and the Right on the political spectrum betokens only the violence of their certitude. Precisely by virtue of that violence, political radicality harbors a deeply conservative motive.

Such conservatism is implicit even in as innocent and 'not inherently exciting a subject' as syntax, which necessitates (one reads with some astonishment) that 'I did as any student of poetics would do: I went to see what Mallarmé said about it' (*CD*, 67). The artlessness of this canonical intention implies the possibility that a study of Mallarmé's syntax might be no more justifiable than what Terry Eagleton once called 'another study of Robert Herrick.' Yet, the simplicity of Johnson's introductory sentences to this chapter on syntax is deceptive. Syntax is 'like skin – which, as everyone knows, is a thing that when you have it outside, it helps keep your insides in –, syntax is a thing that when you have it in your surface structure, it helps keep your deep structure deep' (*CD*, 67). Which is to say, syntax prevents that deep structure from surfacing, in turn implying that the actions authorized by speech are also authorized by the repressions made possible by syntax.

If the messages of syntax are thus inscribed on a palimpsest, 'to preserve [an] absence by bringing it to speech,' as Blanchot puts it beautifully,[5] the roots of political radicality are yet deeper and more conservative; for they have their firm anchorings not merely in conserved silences and in their always potentially unwelcome rupturing effects, but in the very repression of this potential.

That this is the deepest, eternal site of the '*penultimate*' (*WD*, 30), where one must follow an imperative not to stop, seems to me most insightfully examined in Johnson's exemplary piece of deconstructive criticism, 'Melville's Fist: The Execution of *Billy Budd*.' With the same provocative conservatism with which she otherwise conscripts Mallarmé's poetry to political action, Johnson conversely announces here that she will examine not the political, the moral, or the legal, or indeed the human, but 'the linguistic implications of [a] murder' (*CD*, 85). These implications rise to the surface when the law requires 'the forcible transformation of ambiguity into decidability' (*CD*, 107). For when the law assumes authority, it must not only interpret the unexamined messages conserved in ambiguity, but it must also forget the repressions by which these interpretations are permitted. The law murders Billy Budd with the violence of its hermeneutical authority. The execution of Billy Budd becomes the execution of *Billy Budd*, the violent closure of an interminable text. Perhaps necessarily, authority invests itself always with lethal finality: 'The final frame of reference is . . . the authority of a sacred text. Authority seems to be nothing other than the vanishing point of textuality' (*CD*, 104).

If interpretative closure always violates textual inderterminacy, if authority is perhaps fundamentally nontextual, reducing to identity what should remain different, Johnson's work could best be summarized as an attempt to delay the inevitable reductionist desire for meaning. The last chapter of *A World of Difference*, entitled 'Apostrophe, Animation, and Abortion,' seems to me Johnson's most brilliant demonstration of the necessity for a revolution in the logic of meaning. The essay is, moreover, an explicit attempt to respond to another essay in the same book, where Johnson chastizes herself as one of the male Yale deconstructionists for failing to include women as authors or critics in her first book. Having there unwittingly perpetuated the 'pseudogenderlessness of language' (*WD*, 41), *A World of Difference* intends 'to undertake the effort . . . required to retrieve [a] lost knowledge' (*WD*, 41).

This lost knowledge is pursued in 'Apostrophe, Animation, and Abortion,' where Johnson undertakes a careful examination of rhetoric as apostrophe, or as address to what is absent or lost. Baudelaire's poem 'Moesta et Errabunda' and Shelley's 'Ode to the West Wind' serve as two famous, figurative examples of a tradition of address that seeks to reanimate a lost self. But if here the distinctions between speaker and addressee allow for the possibility of undoing loss or death, a more literalized version of this situation – where the speaker is a mother and the addressee a dead child – removes the redemptive qualities of figurative language. In a number of moving poetic examples from Gwendolyn Brooks, Lucille Clifton, and Anne Sexton, Johnson demonstrates the impossibility of the mother-as-speaker to remain separate from the object of her address. The woman in Lucille Clifton's 'Lost Baby Poem' (quoted by Johnson) invites 'black men' to call her stranger 'for your never named sake.' The impossibility of naming the lost baby becomes the speaker's own name. The taboo broken by this example may be the illusion of the redemptive quality of language, its power to name. Likewise, the ambiguity of the phrase 'this baby that I bleed' in Anne Sexton's poem, for example, makes it impossible to distinguish violence from victim, subject from object, or self from other. The mother's address to a dead child inverts and literalizes the aestheticization of loss in the history of lyrical poetry. If Johnson sees that history as 'the fantastically intricate history of endless elaborations and displacements of the single cry, "Mama!" ' (WD, 199), then in the mother's voice the fabric of those displacements and repressions has been torn.

Finally, Johnson's own vision here literalizes, I think, Derrida's uncanny announcement of 'a birth . . . in the offing . . . under the species of the nonspecies, in the formless, mute, infant, and terrifying form of monstrosity.' Such fearful intimations of a fundamental lack, loss, or absence beyond the illusory structures which always defer that nothing compel Derrida to confess his reluctant complicity with those who 'turn their eyes away when faced by the as yet unnameable.'[6] The point of Johnson's essay seems to be that such turning away may be possible only for speakers whose relationship to the object of their loss can be objectified, aestheticized, and displaced.

The linguistic predicament announced in the introduction of *The Critical Difference* as 'the oversights and slip-ups that structure our lives' and which amount in

both books to the proverbial 'error we call life' (*CD*, xii)
must attend any effort to attain knowledge. For how,
given Johnson's Freudian notion of language as a structure of inevitable and violent repression, can we at the
same time speak and be conscious of the losses inherent
in speaking? Short of becoming a psychoanalytical discourse on the couch, all that the essays in *A World of
Difference* can examine, therefore, is how 'the existing
patterns of culture and language' and of 'Western discourse' might strategically structure our knowledge to
legitimate its repressions. The only way these repressions can be unmasked as such, as Johnson's essay on
apostrophe, animation, and abortion movingly demonstrates, is through the transcendent experience of suffering. Only through suffering, in other words, can the
transference from linguistic universality to issues in the
real world be tragically complete.

Harold Schweizer

II

In the following lectures, Barbara Johnson looks closely
at texts that have strategically or unwittingly, affirm-
atively or polemically, personified and allegorized deconstruction. Is deconstruction dead? Was it ever alive? Is
the wake of deconstruction a mixture of lamentation and
merry-making before the burial of the corpse, the track
of a moving ship, or the turbulent air left by moving
aircraft or, perhaps, by the ascent of Sir Joshua Reynolds's allegorical embodiment of theory as a young
woman?[7] What gives these questions their timely urgency is the continuing determination by journalistic
commentators to misrepresent, to misread, or not to
read the writings by such theorists of reading as Jacques
Derrida and Paul de Man and the determination of

feminist and other politically engaged writers to assert disabling consequences for activism of the reflexivity, difficulty, and uncertainty that deconstructive reading promotes. Strangely, the celebration of ambiguity and other forms of polysemy in contemporary literary theory has been persistently falsified as a denial of meaning.

Death and exhumation, no less than memory and re-writing, are recurring concerns in the first lecture, giving it a personal immediacy that may surprise readers who have mistakenly thought that deconstruction denies not only meaning but also the humanity of writers and readers. It may be initially tempting to counter such errors with the claim that only in death do the multi-plicity of meaning and the alterities of human subjects subside. But the deaths of Paul de Man and Mary Joe Frug – and especially their aftermaths – make such a claim highly suspect. Not even death brings an end to difference. A student and friend of Paul de Man's, Bar-bara Johnson was no less shaken than Derrida by the posthumous revelation of de Man's anti-Semitic, colla-borationist essays. The discovery of those fragments of de Man's 'past' provided the occasion for an attempted destruction of his reputation and influence in the popu-lar press. In a very different case of 'double death,' Mary Joe Frug, who was a feminist law professor, was brutally murdered in Cambridge at the time she was writing 'A Postmodern Feminist Legal Manifesto.' Although she did not know Professor Frug very well personally, Bar-bara Johnson was invited to respond to her manifesto, which was left unfinished in mid-sentence by her mur-der.[8] Amidst considerable controversy and editorial re-sistance, Frug's text, along with commentaries by Barbara Johnson, Ruth Colker, and Martha Minow, was published in the *Harvard Law Review*. Those texts – as well as feminism, postmodernism, and even Frug's mur-der – were later grotesquely parodied in the annual *Harvard Law Revue*. Perhaps what was so threatening to the young lawyers, who resorted to posthumous sexual harassment, and to several major journalists, who attempted to subject de Man to a second death, was that they found themselves caught precisely at the point where deconstructive reading and political critique (or legal discourse) converge. Both modes of critique, Johnson argues, 'analyze social and intellectual phenomena within concepts of meaning-effects and agency-effects that do not necessarily coincide with the concept of meaning and agency as individual intention.' But Johnson sees a further similarity between the cases of de Man and Frug. In their arrogance and 'precocious sense of entitlement' the young de Man and the students who parodied Frug's work and murder failed to imagine themselves 'in the place of the violated other.'

In her second lecture, 'Women and Allegory,' Johnson continues her investigation of efforts to personify deconstruction (and theory) by considering allegorical representations of theory as a woman. She begins this project with a witty discussion of Reynolds's painting of *Theory*, which is a rare Enlightenment revival of a Renaissance topos and includes the puzzling motto 'THEORY is the Knowledge of what is truly NATURE.' Among the many stunning surprises in this lecture are the intertextual relationships Johnson uncovers between Reynolds's painting, de Man's discourse on eloquence and the epistemology of metaphor, and Derrick Bell's allegorical text *And We Are Not Saved* (1987), which reflects on the failures of the civil rights movement in the United States. (Bell, the first black professor to receive tenure at Harvard Law School, was forced to resign his appointment when his one-man strike against Harvard to demand that an African-American woman be hired and given tenure there reached the two-year limit allowed for leaves of absence.)

The difference between symbol and allegory, which is at stake here, may initially seem (like syntax) not to be inherently interesting or important. Symbol, as de Man argued in 'The Rhetoric of Temporality,' requires a sense of identity of the sign with its referent, as though the sign had the mysterious power to make the referent present. Allegory, on the other hand, rejects such a nostalgia for metaphysical origin, from which it distances itself by always recalling a text that precedes it, just as Reynolds's *Theory* recalls Ripa's, and Bell's recalls Bunyan's *Pilgrim's Progress*. Allegory, on the other hand, refuses to forget the aporia that joins even as it divides knowledge and value; and it insists on recalling the fundamental scandal of language, which is that signs can neither avoid referentiality nor be referentially reliable. Johnson shows, however, that this distinction in rhetorical theory has important and unavoidable consequences for identity politics and for legal discourse. Like the list of characters in Bunyan's narrative – Christian, Faithful, Mr Blind-Man, and Mr No-Good – the membership of the ad hoc committee proposed by some at Harvard to review the *Review's* revue – a black, an Asian, a lesbian, and so on – presumed the possibility of reading and speaking 'as a' black, an Asian, a lesbian, and the rest. If the semiotics of language and the alterity of human subjectivity make such identifications both unavoidable and unstabilizable, what chance is there for sorting the true from the false and the right from the wrong?

Returning to Reynolds's *Theory* at the end of her lecture, Johnson does not want to forget its modest role, however unintentional, in shaping cultural messages that have been injurious to women (and to men). But her employment of de Man's theory of allegory does, nevertheless, raise some suspicion about her earlier reading of the picture. Although it might be objected that Diotima, the teacher of Socrates, according to the *Symposium*, was the mother of philosophy (and perhaps of theory), Socrates only tells Diotima's story in the privacy of Athens's equivalent of a gentlemen's club when few are sober enough to be able to remember the story. Johnson refuses to forget that women are still condemned to wear the veil of allegory when they enter the public space, and even then they are likely to be subject to misogynistic parody.

Michael Payne

NOTES

1   Barbara Johnson, 'Writing', in *Critical Terms for Literary Study*, ed. Frank Lentricchia and Thomas McLaughlin (Chicago: University of Chicago Press, 1990), p. 41.

2   Barbara Johnson, *The Critical Difference: Essays in the Contemporary Rhetoric of Reading* (Baltimore: Johns Hopkins University Press, 1980); *idem, A World of Difference* (Baltimore: Johns Hopkins University Press, 1987). These books are abbreviated *CD* and *WD* respectively.

3   Christopher Norris, review of *The Critical Difference* by Barbara Johnson, *Modern Language Review* 78, no. 2 (April 1983), p. 383.

4   Brook Thomas writes in a similar context: 'Thinking we are encountering something outside of ourselves . . . we end up merely discovering "the other" within ourselves, a discovery that could be described as the most imperialistic of all, since what was once thought to be truly different, is now absorbed into a system that accounts for its own decentering. In the meantime, "the other" seems to be of interest only in so far as it can help . . . in its task of self-definition' ('Preserving and Keeping Order by Killing Time in *Heart of Darkness*,' in *Heart of Darkness: A Case Study in Contemporary Criticism*, ed. Ross C. Murfin (New York: St Martin's Press, 1989), p. 244.

5   Maurice Blanchot, *The Gaze of Orpheus and Other Literary Essays*, trans. Lydia Davis (New York: Station Hill, 1981), p. 120.

6   Jacques Derrida, *Writing and Difference*, trans. Alan Bass (Chicago: University of Chicago Press, 1978), p. 293.

7 For a reproduction of this painting, which Johnson dis-
   cusses in the second lecture, see the cover of this book.
8 'A Postmodern Feminist Legal Manifesto (An Unfinished
   Draft),' *Harvard Law Review*, 105, no. 5 (March 1992),
   pp. 1045–75. Frug's text is principally concerned with the
   violence done to women by legal discourse and its consequences.

Double Mourning and the Public Sphere

Was it a vision, or a waking dream?
  Fled is that music: – Do I wake or sleep?
                            Keats, 'Ode to a Nightingale'

The coffin, a triumph of the illusionist's art . . . had been
removed from the hardware premises of Oetzmann and
Nephew, a noted house of the gonemost west, which in
the natural course of all things continues to supply
funeral requisites of every needed description.
                            Joyce, *Finnegans Wake*

'D'ye see him?' cried Ahab; but the whale was not yet
in sight.
'In his infallible wake, though; but follow that wake,
that's all.'
                            Melville, *Moby Dick*

1 DEATH AND PROSOPOPOEIA IN PAUL DE MAN

Some time after I announced the title of these lectures,
I received a letter from a critic who was compiling ref-
erences to the figure of death in discussions of deconstruction, asking me whether my title could be construed
as such a reference. For ease of reply, he requested that

I simply respond 'yes' or 'no' on the self-addressed post-card he had enclosed. I, reflecting that I had indeed wanted to allude to a service held for the not-yet-buried dead, but also to the expanding wedge of ruffled water that results from the passage of a ship (or whale) and also, somewhat less grammatically, to a state of nonsleep,[1] wrote on the postcard, 'Yes and no (what else?).' Soon afterward, I received another note from him requesting permission to quote 'Yes and no (what else?)' as an epigraph to an essay of his entitled 'Double Reading: Post-Modernism after Deconstruction.'[2] Thus, my throwaway scribble had come back as a quotation, as my property, defamiliarized and public. In its own very minor way, this purloined postcard enacts the structure I will analyze today: the structure of a return of writing in the context of death, or, more precisely, the relation between writing, a redoubling of mourning, and the public sphere.

The critic Jeffrey Nealon did indeed begin his first essay, 'Deconstruction, it seems, is dead in literature departments today.'[3] And in speaking of 'the wake of deconstruction,' I, too, appear to endorse the possibility of describing a literary theory as an entity capable of death – that is, capable of life. What does it mean to treat a theory as an animate being? More precisely, what does it mean to personify deconstruction as animate only by treating it as dead, giving it life only in the act of taking that life away? What is the connection between personification and death? Will deconstruction, like Finnegan, wake up during its own wake?

Rumors about the death of deconstruction, however, have always already been exaggerated. As early as 1980, Vincent Leitch, in a paper appended to his book *Deconstructive Criticism: An Advanced Introduction*, announced, 'No longer busy being born, deconstruction is busy dying.'[4] Yet to judge from certain critics of the literary academy in the United States, deconstruction is not only not dead, it has taken over the minds and perverted the standards of higher education in the United States. Nevertheless, reports of its demise continue to be published within the academy: books with such titles as *Beyond Deconstruction, Against Deconstruction, Consequences of Theory*, and *In the Wake of Theory* are as numerous as reports in the popular press that the values of Western civilization are being 'deconstructed.' How can something so long-standingly moribund continue to have so robustly unwelcome a life?

One answer, perhaps, is the way in which death functions rhetorically *within* deconstructive analyses. Roland Barthes coined the phrase 'The Death of the Author' to describe the post-structuralist critique of the notion of authorial intention. Jacques Derrida has attempted to reread and revalue the association of speech with life and writing with death, demonstrating that even 'living' speech is based on a split between signifiers and signifieds, on self-difference and deferral (*différance*) rather than immediacy. In other words, rather than beaming 'live' meanings directly from one mind to another, speakers, like writers, use a conventional, external ('dead') system of signs (language) that must be learned and deciphered. Derrida pursues the analysis of this 'différance' constitutive of the human even in contexts where it is the mind itself that is being described, finding 'writing' to be the central figure Freud uses to describe the functioning of the mental apparatus.

In a short essay entitled 'A Note Upon the 'Mystic Writing Pad','[5] Freud compares the mind to what, in my childhood, was known as a 'magic slate.' Like the magic slate, the mind is composed of a layer of protection against direct contact with stimuli (the transparent celluloid sheet), a layer of responsiveness (perception-consciousness, the thin translucent sheet), and a layer that can retain permanent traces (memory, equivalent to the dark wax surface on which the other two sheets rest). In his analysis of Freud's analogy, Derrida writes:

No doubt life protects itself by repetition, trace, *différ-ance* (deferral). But we must be wary of this formulation: there is no life present *at first* which would *then* come to protect, postpone, or reserve itself in *différance*. The latter constitutes the essence of life. . . . Life must be thought of as trace before Being may be determined as presence. This is the only condition on which we can say that life *is* death, that repetition and the beyond of the pleasure principle are native and congenital to that which they transgress.[6]

In other words, without memory, both conscious and unconscious, human beings could hardly be what they are. But with memory as its ever more complex constitutive structure – the structure that underlies learning, loving, and loss – the 'living' psyche derives its specificity from its own 'dead' traces.

For Paul de Man, the association between 'death' and 'linguistic predicaments' was perhaps even more central. As Andrzei Warminski put it in his eulogy for de Man:

But what kept these words ('negativity,' 'rigor,' 'pathos,' etc.) from being generalized into a system and what kept his reading from being rigidified into a merely negative method was the word 'death' which he used as often as, but differently from, the others: more like a punctuation mark or a syntactical break than a semantic unit of meaning. This is the word that kept the others honest.[7]

In a well-known essay, de Man once wrote, 'Nothing can overcome the resistance to theory since theory *is* itself this resistance.'[8] In a similar way, perhaps the death of deconstruction is inescapable because deconstruction makes it impossible to ground thinking in any simple concept of 'life.'

In this lecture I would like first to say a few words about the double death of Paul de Man in connection with the question of writing by, about, or in memory of the dead; then to examine the sort of afterlife that deconstruction seems to have won for itself in the public media, and finally to turn to a second instance of double mourning, a very different instance, in which another putative text from beyond the grave triggers intense and painful controversy in the public sphere.

Paul de Man died twice, two very different deaths. First there was his death from cancer in 1983, accompanied by large numbers of publications by and about him, in his memory, and to his memory. With a certain pathos, people expressed the difficulty of eulogizing someone so inhospitable to pathos, although, as Tobin Siebers noted, '*reading* in de Man's definition always exposes a rhetoric of mourning.'[9] In 1984, barely a month after de Man's death, Jacques Derrida delivered three lectures written out of, and about, mourning and memory, taking many of his reference points from de Man's writings. Focusing on de Man's own interest in epitaphic discourse – indeed, on his theory of autobiography as always in a sense posthumous, written by the subject as dead – Derrida quotes extensively from de Man's essay entitled 'Autobiography as De-Facement.' That essay analyzes the structure of autobiography as a form of prosopopoeia, the fiction of a voice from beyond the grave. De Man cites the discussion in Wordsworth's *Essays on Epitaphs* of epitaphs 'which personate the deceased, and represent him as speaking from his own tomb-stone,' alongside the alternative mode, 'that in which the Survivors speak in their own Persons, [which] seems to me upon the whole greatly preferable.'[10] De Man analyzes the underlying reversibility of the two modes, a reversibility that, in seeming to bring the dead back to life, threatens to strike the living dead:

> The fiction of an apostrophe to an absent, deceased, or voiceless entity . . . posits the possibility of the latter's reply and confers upon it the power of speech . . . The

dominant figure of the epitaphic or autobiographical discourse is, as we saw, the prosopopoeia, the fiction of the voice-from-beyond-the-grave . . . Such chiasmic figures, crossing the conditions of death and life with the attributes of speech and silence . . . evoke the latent threat that inhabits prosopopoeia, namely that by making the death [sic] speak, . . . the living are struck dumb, frozen in their own death.[11]

Lingering in the moment of grief and loss and reflecting on the terms of de Man's discussion, Derrida nevertheless seems to contradict this threat of reversibility when he writes:

Everything remains 'in me' or 'in us,' 'between us,' upon the death of the other. Everything is entrusted *to me*; everything is bequeathed or given *to us*, and first of all *to* what I call *memory*, – to the memory, the place of this strange dative [*à la mémoire*, that is, an apostrophe *to* the dead, which posits the possibility of the latter's reply, etc. – B.J.]. All we seem to have left is memory, since nothing appears able to come to us any longer, nothing is coming or to come, from the other to the present.[12]

But this, of course, is precisely what proved false. Something else *did* come to us from the other, and it really turned out to be other. In the resurfacing of de Man's collaborationist essays, particularly the anti-Semitic one entitled 'The Jews in Contemporary Literature,' the 'me' and the 'us' were forced in new ways into the public sphere by the already public otherness of the lost-again other. Suddenly, de Man no longer belonged to the academy, but to history. And not as a hero, but as a villain. The temptation for anyone who admired and mourned de Man lay in transforming the trauma of de Man's past into mourning for the loss of the idealized de Man or for the internal suffering of a de Man coping silently with the irremediable. As Tobin Siebers puts it in the essay cited above, 'We mourn de Man instead of the Jews.' Is it possible to mourn both? I will return to this question later, but, whatever the complexity of the situation, the danger of confusing the victim with the perpetrator, the slide into a reversibility of their places, is as real as the reversibility of the places of the living and the dead in de Man's discussion of prosopopoeia.

The de Man affair soon produced quite a number of articles and books in both the academic and the popular press, including several efforts of my own.[13] There does not seem to me to be any doubt that the young de Man greeted the 'New World Order' brought by Germany to Europe with overall approval and optimism, at least in the texts he published at the time. I am also convinced that de Man's later work in literary theory is an attempt to combat the mystifications by which he had been se-duced as a young man. Violent disagreement has oc-curred over the question of *judging* de Man. What kind of responsibility should he be expected to bear as an agent, however minor, of the Holocaust? Should he have later publicly acknowledged the existence of the *Le Soir* articles? Do his early collaboration and his silence under-mine the intelligence or value of his later analyses? And if 'death' was the word that kept the others 'honest,' what exactly does 'honest' mean in the case of Paul de Man? Should a theory be judged by the character of the theorist? How can such a 'character' be known? Which de Man are we judging? What de Man can we know? As a literary theorist, I have come to regard 'identity' as a constantly shifting, discontinuous, ungrounded fiction. As a person who trusted, admired, and learned from Paul de Man, I cannot put that last question to rest.

I will return to de Man and his work periodically in these lectures, but here, rather than rehearsing these debates further, I would like to look briefly at the larger public debates over politics in the literary academy, to which the de Man scandal has contributed considerable heat, if not light. In particular, I would like to look at the media's way of linking deconstruction with what critics of the university have called 'political correctness.'

2   DECONSTRUCTION AND POLITICAL CORRECTNESS

In recent attacks on the university, there has been a persistent tendency to link deconstruction with the phenomena of multiculturalism and political correctness. 'Multiculturalism' is the attempt to include within university curricula (as well as within the student body and the faculty) a more diverse selection of works, questions, and approaches than that offered by traditional literary and intellectual canons. 'Political correctness' ('PC') is the name chosen by critics of multiculturalism to attack the ways in which the movement to eliminate racism, sexism, and homophobia has attempted to implement the right to equal access to education. Such attempts to eliminate intolerance have also been called 'the McCarthyism of the left.' The choice of these two expressions is interesting; both involve the transfer of an expression from its original context to an opposite context. McCarthyism was a censorship by the Right of the Left; here, the Right is using the name of its own excesses to distance itself from its history and find its own sins in the other. But in so doing, it is not reversing, but rather repeating, that history. The phrase 'political correctness' came into common usage in the *self*-critiques of various radical movements of the 1970s (the New Left, Black Power, and feminist movements), concerned about the possibility that their critiques of orthodoxy might produce an equally constraining orthodoxy.[14] By co-opting the term, critics of the university are implying that the Left *has* imposed a new orthodoxy, that the

Right is *not* behaving politically, and that the Left is *not* engaged in its own self- critique.

As a way of broaching the question of the relation between deconstruction and the foregoing issues, I will cite three typically garbled media reports, from *Newsweek*, *New York Magazine*, and the *Economist*:

Philosophically, PC represents the subordination of the right to free speech to the guarantee of equal protection under the law. The absolutist position on the First Amendment is that it lets you slur anyone you choose. The PC position is that a hostile environment for minorities abridges their right to an equal education. . . . But solicitude for minorities does not stop at shielding them from insults. Promotion of 'diversity' is one of the central tenets of PC. . . . Politically, PC is Marxist in origin, in the broad sense of attempting to redistribute power from the privileged class (white males) to the oppressed masses. . . . Intellectually, PC is informed by deconstructionism, a theory of literary criticism associated with the French thinker Jacques Derrida. This accounts for the concentration of PC thought in such seemingly unlikely disciplines as comparative literature. Deconstructionism is a famously obscure theory, but one of its implications is a rejection of the notion of 'hierarchy.' It is impossible in deconstructionist terms to say that one text is superior to another. PC thinkers have embraced this conceit with a vengeance.[15]

Deconstruction declared that texts, to use the preferred word, had no meaning outside themselves . . . That being the case, any attempt to assign meaning to art, literature, or thought, to interpret and evaluate it, was nothing more than an exercise in political power by the individual with the authority to impose his or her view. . . . The list of so-called Great Books [is seen] as a propaganda exercise to reinforce the notion of white-male superiority.[16]

What David Lehman's outstanding book demonstrates is that one of the most powerful intellectual movements in American universities is morally bankrupt. It is not just that its prophet, the late Paul de Man, was a Nazi . . . What is more novel and more shocking is the way that his followers and colleagues – particularly Jacques Derrida, the French originator of deconstruction – sought in the late 1980s to use the school's techniques and jargon to obscure the facts of de Man's case and to weasel him out of the charges against him. [Of course, it should be noted that it was Derrida who first brought the wartime writings to public attention – B.J.]

Unlike de Man's hidden fascist past, these recent antics cannot be written off as irrelevant to the theory of deconstruction (and, perhaps, its more recent offshoot, the 'political correctness' movement among America's left-wing academics). . . . The ideas of deconstruction cannot easily be summarized, since they are a mess. The deconstructive approach to a 'text' – which can be a television sitcom or a road sign as easily as an epic poem – is to dismantle it, paying particular attention to its elitist, anti-feminist or otherwise un-chic presuppositions. The enterprise is informed by a philosophy according to which the world is indeterminate until someone – temporarily, and only after a fashion – makes it determinate by using words to describe it. Since words are (allegedly) always shifting their meanings, no interpretation of those words is more correct than any other . . . It is all too easy to see how such ideas led to today's radical critique of the orthodox humanistic canon – the immutable truths to be found in the works of dead white European males . . . According to Mr Lehman, today's 'politically correct' academics come close to embodying a notion of the literary critic as an agent of the thought police.[17]

In these accounts, deconstruction, however 'famously obscure' a 'mess' it may be, seems to be promoting some rather simple and grandiose ideas. But if it were true that 'texts have no meaning,' how would it be possible to say so? Wouldn't such a statement be making an absolute claim to know the meaning of every text (that is, none)?

The same holds for the other claims: 'No text is superior to any other' or 'No interpretation is more correct than any other.' Don't these sentences pose as *the* superior text, *the* correct interpretation? What these caricatures do is to transform the deconstructive *questioning* of absolute claims into new absolute claims. It is as though they are saying that if more than one interpretation is possible, then everything is equally meaningless; if value judgments are open to debate, then they cannot be made; if words sometimes shift in meaning, interpretation becomes fruitless rather than all the more necessary; if analysis is an interminable process of struggle and debate, it's not worth starting. It is as though thinking, reading, and interpreting are only worth undertaking if we know in advance that we will come to rest in absolute, timeless, universal truth.

As a juxtaposition of the two uses of the word 'correct' in the third quotation above will suggest, the descriptions of political correctness are also internally contradictory. Proponents of political correctness are said not to believe in the possibility of correctness ('No interpretation of those words is more *correct* than any other'). PC thinkers are said to have no standards and to have the wrong standards. They have no morals, and they act like a moral thought police. Deconstruction and political correctness are thus attacked for both an insufficiency and an excess of judgment, for seeing at once no meaning and an all too predictable meaning. By linking the critique of the 'white male' canon to the loss of standards, these critics imply, perhaps unwittingly, that they believe in white male supremacy, or at least that they prefer the concepts of 'superiority' and 'hierarchy' to the concepts of 'justice' or 'equality.' It is as if the act of saying that the values of the 'orthodox humanistic canon' are related to the power and interests of the dominant classes of Europeans is a mere power play based on no values; as if to measure the West against its *own* values – or to measure a text against its own evidence – were to reject, dismiss, or pervert it.

These linkages between deconstruction and 'political correctness' are ill-informed attempts to get at something that is actually new and true about literary studies. On the surface, of course, these accounts are reductive and inaccurate: first, because the work of Jacques Derrida and Paul de Man (two white males) deals almost exclusively with writings by canonical white male authors – Plato, Hegel, Rousseau, Wordsworth, Yeats, Heidegger, Husserl, Kant, Proust, Shelley (Percy, not Mary), Pascal, Descartes, Mallarmé, Baudelaire, and so forth. In fact, the work of Derrida could be said to constitute a rereading of precisely those 'Great Books' that the critics of the university claim no one is being encouraged to read any more. De Man would have been very surprised indeed to find himself described as anti-elitist and feminist. On some level, whatever the outcome of a deconstructive reading, the fact that the Western 'Great Books' are still the texts of reference only confirms their authority and importance. As Molefi Asante writes in *The Afrocentric Idea*:

> Eurocentric critics cannot neutralize their cultural 'superiority' when they criticize previous white critics or engage in criticism themselves. The deconstructionists come close to redesigning the critical framework, although much of what they do falls squarely within the context of the Eurocentric theoretical framework. . . . In this regard, the deconstructionists are like the Sierra Club in Kenya or the Red Cross in South Africa; their jobs depend on the mistakes of others. An imperial ideology creates the need for missionaries and Red Cross workers.[18]

Far from undermining the Western canon, deconstruction has given that canon new life.

The media accounts are also reductive in a second way: they neglect the fact that, *within* the academy, deconstruction and political critique are often at odds. Whereas critics in the public media are attacking deconstruction for its subversive politics, politically radical critics of deconstruction *within* the academy have long attacked it for its quietistic, apolitical neutrality, its inaptitude to lead to political intervention, its privileging of analysis over action. Because deconstruction involves the analysis of texts or situations to the point of 'aporia' or 'undecidability,' the argument goes, it paralyzes, or at least cannot authorize, action.

Particularly in the case of 'identity politics,' deconstruction has been seen by critics as undermining, rather than enabling, political agency. Thus Bella Brodzki and Celeste Schenck write:

> The issue of identity is precisely the ground on which feminism and deconstruction part company, for deconstruction aims to undo essential selfhood where feminism recognizes the political necessity of affirming subjective agency. In deconstruction, identity has no priority or authority; subjectivity is the inevitable aftermath of a play of cultural forces; it never precedes, but is only constituted in language. Feminist critics who have worked to theorize a female subject, like Nancy K. Miller or Teresa de Lauretis, do so because even if representation is only a fiction, it is a necessary illusion upon which men have capitalized for centuries and to which women currently view access as crucial.[19]

While Derrida has often spoken of 'woman' or 'the margin' or 'difference' as a structure the repression of which has underpinned Western logocentrism ('orthodox humanism'), his reversal and displacement of binary oppositions (male/female, center/margin, speech/writing, identity/difference, and so on) often occur in philosophical or figurative, rather than historical or political, terms, although his increasing attention to the rhetorical and historical nature of *institutions* renders that opposition problematic. But in seeing the notions of identity, self-presence, and intentionality as *inherently* repressive of internal differences, Derrida renders epistemologically groundless *all* identities, even those of women or racial minorities who would attempt to assert themselves oppositionally. Thus, while Derrida's analyses carry with them a clear imperative against structures of domination, he also finds and critiques such structures when they are repeated within the very premises of many liberation movements. In this sense, while political activists are critiquing deconstruction for analyzing the world without intervening to change it, deconstruction is warning against the identity-based grounds on which such an intervention has been conceptualized.

Why, then, would anyone want to give deconstruction the blame – or the credit – for having opened up questions of politics or cultural diversity within the teaching of the humanities? How could the careful reading of a classic text possibly lead to the undermining of the values of Western civilization?

Actually, the latter is precisely what de Man claims in his essay 'The Return to Philology.' In that essay, he describes the pedagogy he learned from Reuben Brower:

> No one could be more remote from high-powered French theory than Reuben Brower. . . . Brower, however, believed in and effectively conveyed what appears to be an entirely innocuous and pragmatic precept . . . Students, as they began to write on the writings of others, were not to say anything that was not derived from the text they were considering. They were not to make any statements that they could not support by a specific use of language that actually occurred in the text. They were asked, in other words, to begin by reading texts closely as texts and not to move at once into the general context of human experience or history. Much more humbly or modestly, they were to start out from the bafflement that such singular turns of tone,

phrase, and figure were bound to produce in readers attentive enough to notice them and honest enough not to hide their non-understanding behind the screen of received ideas that often passes, in literary instruction, for humanistic knowledge . . . Mere reading, it turns out, prior to any theory, is able to transform critical discourse in a manner that would appear deeply subversive to those who think of the teaching of literature as a substitute for the teaching of theology, ethics, psychology, or intellectual history. Close reading accomplishes this often in spite of itself because it cannot fail to respond to structures of language which it is the more or less secret aim of literary teaching to keep hidden.[20]

Expanding upon the 'reading in slow motion' taught by Brower in a Harvard humanities course for which de Man was a teaching fellow in the 1950s, de Man implicitly describes his own reading practice in the 1980s, which extends Brower's attention to language in the direction of a more systematic study of rhetoric. Several things can be said about the passage I have just quoted. First, by cautioning the student not to move 'at once' to the context of human history, de Man would seem to be arguing against the direct politicizing of the literary text. But second, the word 'subversive' is used to describe mere close reading. While critics of the university are claiming that campus radicals are subverting the literary canon and that students are no longer reading it, de Man is here claiming that really *reading* the canon is what is subversive, because students in traditional 'humanist' classrooms are usually taught *not* to read it but to learn ideas about it. And second, this subversiveness arises out of attention to the structures of language. Language does things in texts, de Man suggests, that resist absorption into the screen of received ideas. Language can produce bafflement, non-understanding. Students become better readers if they pay attention to their own *non*-understanding. The text contains resistance to mere ideas, cannot be simply translated into ideas, results, conclusions.

This, of course, goes against the grain of many reigning pedagogical assumptions. And the slow reading de Man describes here does not carry with it a justification through practical or political usefulness. Indeed, he says that writing about texts becomes more difficult in this process: 'The profession is littered with the books that the students of Reuben Brower failed to write.' What, then, is the use of this slow reading? Simply that it refuses to hide its non-understanding, its encounter with the text as other. Students who learn not to seek the text's meaning in existing authoritative pronouncements about it, but rather in their own relationship and struggle with it, will have to encounter the unprepackagedness of evidence. They will develop better skills as readers by not backing away from the text, by not assuming that what they don't understand will be clarified by someone else's more authoritative reading.

It would seem, then, that the liberation of the reader from the screen of received ideas about meaning and from the system of projections about intention occurs through a hyper-fidelity to the language of the text. If the reader's authority to read is to develop other than through the screen of received ideas, then the authority previously located in the teacher or in the intellectual tradition is transferred to the reader, but only by way of the text. To suspend the context of human experience or history, not to move to such a context *at once*, is to take the text's language seriously *no matter what*.

But the pedagogical context and discipline that surrounds the exercise of hyper-fidelity may contain its own imperatives and prohibitions. If we turn back to de Man's description of learning to read subversively, we can hear the ways in which the authority of the institution is nevertheless maintained. The instructions to the students are phrased in the grammar of an absolute but hidden authority: 'Students were not to . . . they were to . . .' I would like now to quote the different spin Richard Ohmann gives to a very similar scene of reading in his 1976 study *English in America*:

> Another thing a student is supposed to be is objective. The Acorn Book says that his Advanced Placement English course will teach him how to read *and respond* to works of literature, but if the descriptive material and the examinations are any indication, the Advanced Placement Program actually teaches the student *not* to respond to literature, not with his feelings. His concern must be with 'organization of the elements of the poem,' with 'particular uses of language' that express a contrast, with the function of minor characters, with the way structure, imagery, and sound contribute to the whole meaning of a poem – 'Your feeling about the poem is important,' he is implicitly told, 'only as the outcome of careful reading.' His role is that of the neutral instrument, recording and correlating the facts and drawing conclusions. If any need or interest *other* than the formalistic drove him to read the work, or indeed, if something within turns him *against* the work, he will quickly learn to suppress these unwelcome responses. They are not among the competencies that will move him a step up the ladder. To his reading of a poem he is supposed to bring the techniques he has mastered, and only those. He is, in other words, alienated in very nearly the Marxian sense. And, of course, the ideal student is of the middle class. Docility, care, tidiness, professional ambition, the wish for objectivity, these are all qualities valued particularly by the middle class and encouraged in its young.[21]

I would like to let the de Man quotation and the Ohmann quotation stand as representatives of the two sides of the subtitle to this section, 'Deconstruction and Political Correctness,' or rather, 'political critique'; as the two *different* ways in which classical deconstruction

and classical ideological criticism question the authority
of the institution of literary studies on its own grounds
– what reading is – and serve as critiques of each other.
The Ohmann quotation reveals the extent to which the
student's emotive and political reality is repressed and
subordinated to a neutralized formalism. But if the student *does* respond with feelings, 'he' may stop reading
what the text actually says or reduce the text to a projection. In enjoining the student to *stay with* the text, not
to move *at once* to the historical or personal context, de
Man urges a suspension of projection and resolution out
of respect for the otherness of the text. But in doing so,
he absolutizes the text's authority and frame of reference
and reduces the reader to a neutral, impersonal, 'objec-
tive' function of textual structures. Indeed, the subject
of the verb 'respond' in de Man's description is not 'he'
(the reader, as in Ohmann) but 'it' ('Close reading accomplishes this often in spite of itself because *it* cannot
fail to respond to structures of language'). Does the
reader, the subject, have interpretive agency in the reading, or is 'he' the site of a personification, the place
where a more impersonal intellectual process takes place
on its own but often 'in spite of itself'? It would be easy
to dismiss de Man's 'it' as a 'mere' personification, a
false attribution of agency. But since such personifications occur regularly at culminating points in de Man's
arguments, they are clearly carrying an important part
of the thrust of his work. Note, for example, the personification that occurs in the climactic sentence about allegory from 'The Rhetoric of Temporality', to which I
will return in the second lecture: 'Whereas the symbol
postulates the possibility of an identity or identification,
allegory designates primarily a distance in relation to
its own origin, and, *renouncing the nostalgia and the desire
to coincide*, it establishes its language in the void of
this temporal difference.'[22] Some sense of the complexity
of the question of the status of the agency of such

personifications in intellectual and literary history can be gleaned from the uses of such personifications in the attacks on deconstruction and political correctness quoted earlier. In the passage from *New York* we read: '*Deconstruction declared* that texts had no meaning outside themselves.' And in the quotation from the *Economist* we read: 'It is all too easy to see how such *ideas led* to today's radical critique of the orthodox humanistic canon.' One of the tenets of that canon seems to be that 'ideas' can 'lead.' If the personification of 'close reading' or 'allegory' is deemed merely rhetorical, what happens to the leadership of ideas? Or, for that matter, of 'America,' another personification?

I would like to conclude this section with two further quotations which draw out the implications of what it might mean for a reader to respond to a text by *not* taking it on its own terms. As it happens, 'America' is central to both these scenes of reading. First, a now classic feminist analysis:

> American literature is male. Our literature neither leaves women alone nor allows them to participate. It insists on its universality at the same time that it defines that universality in specifically male terms . . . In such fictions the female reader is co-opted into participation in an experience from which she is explicitly excluded; she is asked to identify with a selfhood that defines itself in opposition to her; she is required to identify against herself . . . To be excluded from a literature that claims to define one's identity is to experience a peculiar form of powerlessness – not simply the powerlessness which derives from not seeing one's experience articulated, clarified, and legitimized in art, but more significantly the powerlessness which results from the endless division of self against self, the consequence of the invocation to identify as male while being reminded that to be male – to be universal, to be American – is to be *not female*.[23]

From this quotation, it is clear that literature not only has personified agency ('Our literature neither leaves women alone nor allows them to participate') but that it has powerful designs on the very personhood of the reader ('she is required to identify against herself . . . the endless division of self against self'). The text itself is engaged in what might be called 'gender harassment.' Not only is personification unavoidable in describing this struggle: what it means to be a person, a 'self,' is precisely what is at stake.

Here is my second quotation, taken from a more recent study:

> For some time now I have been thinking about the validity or vulnerability of a certain set of assumptions conventionally accepted among literary historians and critics and circulated as 'knowledge.' This knowledge holds that traditional, canonical American literature is free of, uninformed, and unshaped by the four-hundred-year-old presence of, first, Africans and then African-Americans in the United States. It assumes that this presence – which shaped the body politic, the Constitution, and the entire history of the culture – has had no significant place or consequence in the origin and development of that culture's literature. Moreover, such knowledge assumes that the characteristics of our national literature emanate from a particular 'Americanness' that is separate from and unaccountable to this presence. There seems to be a more or less tacit agreement among literary scholars that, because American literature has been clearly the preserve of white male views, genius, and power, those views, genius, and power are without relationship to and removed from the overwhelming presence of black people in the United States. This agreement is made about a population that preceded every American writer of renown and was, I have come to believe, one of the most furtively radical impinging forces on the country's literature. The contemplation of this black presence is central to any understanding of

our national literature and should not be permitted to hover at the margins of the literary imagination.

These speculations have led me to wonder whether the major and championed characteristics of our national literature – individualism, masculinity, social engagement versus historical isolation; acute and ambiguous moral problematics; the thematics of innocence coupled with an obsession with figurations of death and hell – are not in fact responses to a dark, abiding, signing Africanist presence.[24]

Unlike the gender harassment described above by Judith Fetterley, the racial harassment described here by Toni Morrison occurs not by direct scapegoating but by omission, erasure, false completeness. From these two quotations, it becomes clear that the text may itself be a 'response' to the reader it represses, marginalizes, or excludes. While the 'close reading' de Man recommends is an act of respect for, and receptiveness to, the text itself, it cannot give access to what the text denies, excludes, or distorts. While not hiding one's non-knowledge may be a way of avoiding projection, treating the text as all-knowing disregards the ways in which the *text's* blindnesses may be historical and political rather than structural and essential. The close reading that de Man describes neutralizes the ways in which the text and the reader are *both* participants in a field of struggle. But it does bring out the ways in which such a struggle takes place as much among personifications as among persons.

3   PROSOPOPOEIA AND FREE SPEECH

While literary studies can be described as being in, or at, the wake of deconstruction, there are other domains in which deconstruction can also be said to have made waves: architecture, fashion design, and especially law, where deconstruction has had a career equal in controversy and importance to the career it has had in literary studies, particularly through the work of what has been called Critical Legal Studies. The Critical Legal Studies movement, which took shape during the 1970s, has been described by Mark Tushnet as loosely organized around 'three propositions about law: that it is in some interesting sense indeterminate; that it can be understood in some interesting way by paying attention to the context in which legal decisions are made; and that in some interesting sense law is politics.'[25] Critical Legal Studies thus brings together the questions raised by deconstruction and political critique.

In the fall of 1991, I was asked by the *Harvard Law Review* to serve as one of three respondents to an essay left unfinished at the death of its author. The other two respondents were Ruth Colker (professor of law, Tulane University) and Martha Minow (professor of law, Harvard). Entitled 'A Postmodern Feminist Legal Manifesto,'[26] the essay was written by Mary Joe Frug, a professor at the New England School of Law, who had recently been brutally murdered on a Cambridge street not far from her home. I had met Mary Joe occasionally at 'law and literature' gatherings but did not know her well. She was one of the most engaging voices among the 'Fem Crits' – the feminist scholars whose work was both informed by, and critical of, Critical Legal Studies. The Fem Crits, too, saw the law as shaped by the interests of those in power; but they also pointed out ways in which 'among CLS proponents, the concerns of the racially and sexually subordinated were both recognized and marginalized.'[27] Despite my lack of legal credentials, I undertook to respond to Mary Joe Frug both out of a sense of loss at her death and out of a somewhat masochistic curiosity about the law journal editorial process I had read about in the work of Patricia Williams.[28]

Frug's essay concerns ways in which legal rules combine to maternalize, terrorize, and sexualize the female body so that heterosexual monogamy appears to be a woman's safest life choice. This is another way of saying that law is inseparable from patriarchy. Not only was her essay itself unfinished at the time of her death; she got up to go out for her fatal walk in the middle of a sentence. Here is the sentence:

> Women who might expect that sexual relationships with other women could

The sentence dangles in the middle of the essay, which continues for another nine pages.

Now my assignment was to read the text. Critics of literary theory have attacked the concept of the death of the author, especially Paul de Man's statement that 'death is a displaced name for a linguistic predicament,'[29] but here I precisely *encountered* Mary Joe Frug's death as a linguistic predicament. In my commentary, I wrote about this sentence, calling it 'the lesbian gap' and asking, 'How does this gap signify?' I sent my commentary to the *Harvard Law Review* for its round of editorial responses. When it came back from its first reading, the editors had changed 'How does this gap signify?' to 'What does this gap mean?' This is not at all the same question. '*What* does the gap mean?' implies that it *has* a meaning and that all I have to do is to figure out what it is. 'How does the gap *signify*?' implies that it may generate interpretive *effects* without necessarily 'having' *a* meaning. '*How* does the gap signify?' raises the *question* of what it means to mean, raises meaning as a question, implies that the gap *has to be read*, but that it can't be presumed to have been intended. The 'death of the author' names the unknowability of the gap between what a text says and what an author might have intended, even when the author is not literally dead.

Again, it is a questioning of the self-presence implied by the concept of 'life' as 'meaning.' The *Law Review* responded as if to question the mode or possibility of meaning was to speak a foreign language. In every successive revision that my text underwent, the *how* was again changed to *what*. From this I learned that law review writing is a resistance to opening up meaning as a question, as a non-given, as a bafflement, as the possibility that what is intended and what is readable might not be the same. In another symptomatic revision, the editors changed my claim that Mary Joe Frug 'encountered an impossibility' to 'she became skeptical,' thus locating the intellectual event *within* consciousness. And in my concluding sentence I had written (using a phrase Frug had used in the essay: 'I note the discomfort and go on'): 'She notes the discomfort, the fascination, the terror, but could not go on.' The editors queried the discrepancy between the tenses, changing 'notes' to 'noted.' But the discrepancy between Frug's writing – which can be described in an eternal present – and Frug's career – cut short just as it was coming into its own – was what I wanted to capture through the 'agrammaticality.' The ideology of law review style would thus seem to attempt to create a world saturated with meaning, intention, and consciousness – without discontinuities or gaps.

In my reading, I connected the 'lesbian gap' to two other points at which Frug's argument breaks off – though not in the middle of a sentence. In each of the other two cases, Frug has come up against the fact that feminists disagree among themselves. She describes the disagreements, does not choose a side, and then describes the debate itself as a form of resistance to the dominance of patriarchy as usual. The complete form of the 'lesbian gap' on the page, similarly, is as follows:

Women who might expect that sexual relationships with other women could

[to be completed by:
economic and security incentives that make a male partner more advantageous for non-sexual reasons than a
same-sex partner for women

In other words, in all three cases, the discontinuity occurs over the question of women's relations to each
other, and the text leaps in each case to the more familiar
topic of women facing men. In this way, Mary Joe Frug's
text remains within the discourse of compulsory hetero-
sexuality. The 'lesbian gap' is not an isolated and entire-
ly contingent accident: it is part of a logic of repetition
in the essay. And my reading assumes that a gap can be
read, not by filling it with meaning but by finding the
logic of the text to which it contributes, by assuming that
the text has its own dynamic – even a text broken by the
seemingly contingent accident of death. This is one way
to answer the question 'How does the gap signify?'

There are other ways. Certainly, as a lesbian, I read
the unfinished sentence with astonishment. What was
Mary Joe imagining/repressing/fearing/desiring? Did she
decide to go to the store because she had too many ideas
or too few? Was she afraid she wouldn't get it right? The
fact that we will never know the answer to these questions does not prevent me from asking them, but it does
require me to read otherwise. One of the other commentators on her essay, Ruth Colker, pursued the question
of the relevance of Frug's text to lesbians in a different
way. She showed the ways in which some of Frug's
generalizations about what 'legal rules' do to women
don't apply to lesbians. While Frug claims that 'women'
are legally maternalized, for example, Colker points out
that lesbians are often legally *dematernalized*, prevented
from having custody of their own children. What might
seem like a biological given – motherhood – turns out to
be a cultural construction tied to the control of women
by men. Colker's analysis bears out Frug's general point

that women's bodies are culturally constructed by law, but by turning Frug's text against itself. Despite her intentions, Mary Joe Frug's generalizations about 'women' make lesbians vanish. This is another way in which the text contains a 'lesbian gap.' It is also a way in which Frug enacts her own claims about the necessity of recognizing the 'incoherence' of the word 'woman.'

One of the most striking rhetorical features of the commentaries of both Ruth Colker and Martha Minow is their decision to address Mary Joe Frug directly. Ruth Colker's text begins:

> How do you respond to an unfinished manuscript written by a friend who was tragically murdered less than one year ago when you continue to see images of her sitting on a couch talking to you juxtaposed with images of her lying dead on a street in Cambridge? The manuscript is filled with images of violence and death, as if Mary Joe were foreshadowing her own passing from this world. I want to talk to Mary Joe about the manuscript. What did you mean, here and there? How were you intending to finish it? What troubled you about it that you intended to revise?[30]

And Martha Minow's entire commentary is written in the form of 'An Unsent Letter to Mary Joe Frug' and begins: 'Dear Mary Joe.'

Direct address is the most effective way of treating Mary Joe Frug as alive. As Paul de Man wrote in the passage quoted earlier, 'The fiction of an apostrophe to an absent, deceased, or voiceless entity . . . posits the possibility of the latter's reply and confers upon it the power of speech.' The transference of speech from the living to the dead institutes a rhetorical reversibility that is enacted in Colker's use of 'you' both for herself and for Mary Joe in her opening and by her reference to her own reply as 'posthumous.' But the inverse of apostrophe, prosopopoeia, the fiction of the voice-from-beyond-the-grave, is in fact evoked in the editors' note that precedes the publication of Mary Joe Frug's 'Postmodern Feminist Legal Manifesto' itself. In the *Harvard Law Review*, Frug's essay is prefaced as follows:

> The following commentary is an unfinished work. Professor Frug was working on this Commentary when she was murdered on April 4, 1991. The Editors of the *Harvard Law Review* agreed that, under the circumstances, the preservation of Mary Joe Frug's voice outweighed strict adherence to traditional editorial policy. For this reason, neither stylistic nor organizational changes have been made, and footnotes have been expanded but not added.[31]

What can be said about this departure from the usual editorial procedures? It seems that it is only when the author is dead that a law review sees value in the preservation of 'voice.' What does 'voice' mean here, if not prosopopoeia? Is the 'voice' of an author *always* 'the fiction of the voice-from-beyond-the-grave'? In any event, it seems as though there are two no-win models for authorship here: an interactive editorial process through which a 'living' author participates in the progressive erasure of her own words and a textual respect that can only occur if the author is dead.

But, as an article in *Mirabella* put it, 'Mary Joe Frug was murdered twice.'[32] On 4 April, 1992, on the first anniversary of her death, the *Harvard Law Review* held its annual banquet, during which copies of the editors' annual 'spoof' edition, the *Harvard Law Revue*, were circulated. The 1992 *Revue* contained a parody of Mary Joe Frug's essay entitled 'He-Manifesto of Post-Mortem Legal Feminism,' authored by 'Mary Doe, Rigor-Mortis Professor of Law,' dictated from beyond the grave. Here was prosopopoeia with a vengeance. *With a vengeance.* It seems that, to some members of the editorial board who had opposed the publication of Frug's essay, the author was not quite dead enough. She was still speaking. They had been unable either to silence or even to edit her voice. Indeed, their opposition itself had been erased in the apparent unanimity of the 'Editors' Note' cited above ('The Editors of the HLR agreed . . .') They therefore seem to have decided to turn the fiction of her voice, the instrument of her survival, into a weapon with which to violate her again. And, by extension, to put *all* feminists in their place (the bedroom and the kitchen, according to various footnotes to the text). The authors take their revenge in a number of ways. They make light of Mary Joe's death by seeing it as a ploy to get published ('See M. J. Frug, WHAT'S A GAL GOT TO DO TO APPEAR IN THE *HARVARD LAW REVUE?* (1990) (threatening to hold her breath 'til she turns blue in the face)'[33]). They show her reporting on the afterlife in a breezy, gossipy tone ('Here I was on my first day on Cloud Nine (I must say, these gowns have nothing on Chanel)'[34] or spewing what they take to be postmodern feminist clichés ('No one, as far as I know, has ever tried to deconstruct the Bible.[35] If they did, they would find that Heaven is a sexist, pearly-gates, ivory-towers kind of place'[36]). They respond to the sexually explicit, colloquial language of Frug's essay (which they had attempted to censor in the original publication) as if it were a sexual provocation. In footnote after footnote, they describe their own sexual prowess or frustration. They see feminists as sexually aggressive and powerful; Mary Doe ogles men in Speedos, eats hot dogs, and goes 'out at night to hunt down some hunky men and rip their clothes off'[37]. The victim of sexual violence is thus here confused with the perpetrator: it was Mary Joe who went out at night and encountered the fatal thrusts of a seven-inch knife, gashing her in the chest and groin. By painting feminists as sexually aggressive, the authors of the parody deny the vulnerability of all women, whatever their politics, to sexual violence. And by *sexualizing* feminism, they deny its intellectual, institutional, and political seriousness. They both exaggerate and belittle the power of feminism, parodying the call for diversity by seeing it as the embrace of mediocrity or unattractiveness ('Heaven should be open to everyone. White, Black, Male, Female, Short, Fat, Bald, Talented, Untalented. It's a person's heart and not the hair under her arms that counts'[38]). (Indeed, the image of feminism as the growth of female body hair has become the most effective phobic object that exists in the mainstream media to keep women from identifying with the *word* 'feminist.') The authors of the *Revue* parody also undercut the members of the editorial board who had argued for the publication of Frug's essay by claiming that it had been published only because Frug's husband was a tenured professor at Harvard. The number of disparaging remarks made in the parody about Gerald Frug by name lead one to suspect that part of its energy results from its status as an oedipal tantrum, designed to 'kill' not a woman but a father figure and to win for the authors a position within the debates among senior men at Harvard. By putting all this in the mouth of the fictional Mary Joe, the parody forces 'her' to betray everything she believed in.

Almost immediately, members of the law school community began to speak out against the gleeful misogyny and desecration involved in the 'spoof.' What seemed appalling was, in the first place, the unfathomable cruelty toward those who still acutely mourned the loss of Mary Joe (what Jerry Frug might have felt had he attended the dinner – to which he *had* been invited – can scarcely be imagined). But even more appalling for their general significance were the attitudes toward women displayed by these future leaders of the legal profession. Was this the result of legal training at one of the country's most prestigious law schools? Were these the men who might some day end up shaping the future direction of justice in America? Many members of the community, both male and female, saw the publication as a symptom of a pervasively hostile or unwelcoming working environment for women at Harvard Law School. Many called for an investigation of how the spoof had been accepted for publication. Some called for its authors to be brought up before the Law School's Administrative Board, which was engaged at that very moment in hearings concerning students who had staged a sit-in for diversity. Why were blatantly demeaning and hurtful words protected when the mere act of occupying the dean's office in the service of a serious cause was punished? Was property really more important than equal opportunity? Was a sit-in 'action,' while an insult was only 'words'?

The call for disciplinary action against the authors of the parody immediately set off an alarm about freedom of speech. Complaints about the 'PC police' transformed the authors of the spoof into the real victims in the case. Professor Alan Dershowitz published an op ed piece in which he described the parody as 'sophomoric' and 'in somewhat poor taste,' the outcry over its publication as an 'overreaction,' and the atmosphere at Harvard Law School as that of a 'McCarthyite witchhunt.'[39] Dean Robert Clark issued an open letter deploring the publication of the spoof but refusing to see it as evidence of pervasive sexism at the institution – indeed, referring to the public outcry as proof that the institution was *not* sexist. The authors of the parody issued a public apology, saying that they had 'intended' no harm. Yet clearly the *fact* that they never imagined the reaction they would elicit stands as a sign of the way in which their parody reflects what *they* at least understood as a permissive environment for misogyny.

But such an environment can only do its damage when no one is calling it by its name. The moment it is named, it is disavowed. This puts feminists in a double bind: if they do not speak out against institutional sexism,

sexism continues to blight the working environment for women; the moment they shine the light on a symptom of systemic sexism, everyone within the institution isolates that instance and dissociates from it. The clearer the example, the quicker the dissociation. The more dubious the example, the more the feminists appear to be overreacting.

What light, if any, does this story shed on the issues discussed in the two previous sections of this lecture? Let me draw several connections. In my discussion of the 'gap' in Frug's essay, I have tried to illustrate how one might read and respond to a text in which language is doing something that can't be tied to a conscious intention. In my discussion of the parody, I have tried to describe how the expression of an ideology looks from the point of view of those it seeks to silence, whether consciously or unconsciously. Language as bafflement and language as politics are not identical. They may even be incommensurable; yet they are somehow inseparable. One would probably not be able to exist without the other. And both are different from the transitive, univocal model of language that sees it only as the expression of a conscious intention.

Those who called for an investigation of the climate of sexual harassment at the *Harvard Law Review* were operating on the assumption of a non-individual-intention-based, symptomatic model of speech. That is, even if the individual authors 'meant no harm' or thought their wit would delight anyone who mattered, the harm the parody did inflict was of a piece with a broader pattern of values, habits, and assumptions that needed to be critiqued on the institutional level. Those who saw the authors of the parody as victims and their publication as protected by the First Amendment saw it not as systemic but as private, sophomoric, interpersonally regrettable, and isolated. The resistance to recognizing misogyny as institutional is the *same* resistance as the resistance to questioning individual intention and control in language. This is perhaps where deconstruction and political critique come together. Both analyze social and intellectual phenomena within concepts of meaning-effects and agency-effects that do not necessarily coincide with the concept of meaning and agency as individual intention.

I began this lecture with the assumption that there was an interesting parallel between the case of Paul de Man and the case of Mary Joe Frug. Both were admired and loved; both were deeply mourned; and in both cases, mourners had to confront – though very differently – a second traumatic event which opened up a heated controversy in the public sphere. But I now see another parallel between the two cases that I had not seen before. Paul de Man, writing in his early twenties with a precocious sense of entitlement, served as a mouthpiece for a dominant ideology that belittled, demeaned, excluded, and eventually killed millions of Jews. He did not himself commit murder, but he expressed a complete failure to imagine himself in the place of the other whom he was willing to dismiss from Europe. Is his case different from the case of the authors of the Frug parody, also presumably in their early twenties, also speaking with entitlement, also not murderers, yet refusing to take seriously the magnitude of the problem of violence against women, incapable of imagining themselves in the place of the violated other?

In seeing both de Man and the authors of the parody as 'symptomatic' of a dominant discourse, as aiding and abetting the violence they will not themselves commit, as speaking within a world in which they take upon themselves the right to say who is expendable, I have implied that their writings arise out of a collective, rather than an individual, guilt. Does this mean that individuals cannot be held accountable for the ways in which oppressive ideologies speak through them? By critiquing those who would defend offensive speech on First Amendment grounds for failing to see such speech as systemic, do I have to let the offending speakers off the hook? On the contrary, what is needed is a greater recognition of the intentionality of systemic, institutional cultural discourses. On some level, the authors of the Revue parody *did* intend harm. It was just that it was a harm coded as 'normal' by the discourse in which they were writing. In fact, it is they themselves who have resorted to non-intention (they 'intended no harm') *as a defense*. Doesn't their disavowal of intention belie my equation of their position with a belief in intentionality? If the defenders of individual 'free speech' resort to non-intentionality as a defense, isn't there a possible moral ambiguity inherent in the deconstructive *critique* of intentionality?

Yes and no (what else?). On the one hand, the deconstructive analysis of how language works carries with it no absolute guarantee of moral or political correctness. Denying the indeterminacy of language may serve good causes; reading a text against its own grain may legitimate injustice. But the point of a deconstructive analysis is not to treat intentionality as an 'on–off' switch, but to analyze the functioning of many different, sometimes incommensurable, *kinds* of intentionality. As the defensive recourse to non-intentionality implies, the *denial* of intentionality operates within the same paradigm as the *affirmation* of intentionality. The question is not whether there is or is not conscious individual intention, but rather how intentionality-effects, signifying-effects, are generated or undercut by language and culture, whether or not they are acknowledged. While critiques of deconstructive and political analyses imply that they *diminish* or *remove* meaning, we can see that, on the contrary, they *increase* the modes or structures of meaning. In such analyses, the outcome is not *less* meaning but *more* meaning. It is just that the increase of meaning makes

meaning exceed the boundaries of stable control or co-
herence. It becomes something to be endlessly struggled
over. That struggle is what deconstruction leaves in its
wake.

NOTES

1 The epigraphs, of course, were meant to gloss these three
meanings of the word 'wake' in my title. They are also
three different ways of alluding to the life and work of Paul
de Man. First, he was a major theorist of Romanticism
(and of the rhetorical question); second, he was the
nephew of Hendrik de Man, the Belgian Socialist who
urged King Leopold to capitulate to the Nazis in 1940,
and it was probably through the uncle that Paul de Man
got a job as a regular cultural columnist for a collaborationist newspaper, *Le Soir*, in 1940–2; and third, after he
stopped writing for *Le Soir*, he worked as a translator,
translating *Moby Dick* into Flemish.

2 Forthcoming in Jeffrey T. Nealon, *Double Reading: Post-
Modernism after Deconstruction* (Ithaca, N. Y.: Cornell
University Press, 1993).

3 Jeffrey T. Nealon, 'The Discipline of Deconstruction,'
PMLA 107, no. 5 (October 1992), p. 1266.

4 Vincent B. Leitch, 'Hermeneutics, Semiotics, and Decon-
struction' (1980), printed as an appendix to *Deconstructive
Criticism: An Advanced Introduction* (New York: Columbia
University Press, 1983), p. 262.

5 *The Standard Edition of the Complete Psychological Works of
Sigmund Freud*, ed. James Strachey (London: Hogarth
Press, 1961), vol. XIX, pp. 227–32.

6 Jacques Derrida, 'Freud and the Scene of Writing,' in
Writing and Difference, trans. Alan Bass (Chicago: University of Chicago Press, 1978), p. 203.

7 Andrzei Warminski, 'In Memoriam' in 'The Lesson of
Paul de Man,' ed. Peter Brooks, Shoshana Felman, and
J. Hillis Miller, *Yale French Studies* 69 (1985), p. 13.

8 Paul de Man, *The Resistance to Theory* (Minneapolis: University of Minnesota Press, 1986), p. 19.

9 Tobin Siebers, 'Mourning Becomes Paul de Man,' in *Responses: On Paul de Man's Wartime Journalism*, ed. Werner Hamacher, Neil Hertz, and Thomas Keenan (Lincoln and London: University of Nebraska Press, 1989), p. 363, emphasis mine.

10 William Wordsworth, 'Essay Upon Epitaphs,' in *Wordsworth: Poetry & Prose*, ed. W. M. Merchant (Cambridge, Mass.: Harvard University Press, 1963), p. 616.

11 Paul de Man, 'Autobiography as De-Facement,' in *The Rhetoric of Romanticism* (New York: Columbia University Press, 1984), pp. 75–8.

12 Jacques Derrida, *Memoirs for Paul de Man* (New York: Columbia University Press, 1986, 1989), pp. 32–3.

13 See my preface to the paperback edition of *A World of Difference* (Baltimore: Johns Hopkins University Press, 1988) and my essay 'Poison or Remedy? Paul de Man as Pharmakon,' *Colloquium Helveticum* 11/12 (1990), pp. 7–20.

14 See Ruth Perry's illuminating archeology of the term in 'Historically Correct,' *Women's Review of Books* 9, no. 5 (February 1992), pp. 15–16.

15 *Newsweek*, 24 December, 1990, pp. 52–3.

16 John Taylor, 'Are You Politically Correct?', *New York*, 21 January 1991, p. 36.

17 Review of David Lehman, *Signs of the Times, Economist*, 18 May 1991, p. 95.

18 Molefi Kete Asante, *The Afrocentric Idea* (Philadelphia: Temple University Press, 1987), pp. 164–6.

19 Bella Brodzki and Celeste Schenck, '*Criticus Interruptus*: Uncoupling Feminism and Deconstruction,' in *Feminism and Institutions*, ed. Linda Kauffman (Oxford: Blackwell, 1989), p. 202.

20 Paul de Man, 'The Return to Philology,' in *Resistance to Theory*, pp. 23–4.

21 Richard Ohmann, *English in America* (New York: Oxford University Press, 1976), p. 57.

22 Paul de Man, 'The Rhetoric of Temporality,' in *Blindness and Insight* (Minneapolis: University of Minnesota Press, 1983), p. 207.

23 Judith Fetterley, *The Resisting Reader: A Feminist Approach to American Fiction* (Bloomington and London: Indiana University Press, 1977), pp. xii–xiii.

24 Toni Morrison, *Playing in the Dark: Whiteness and the Literary Imagination* (Cambridge, Mass.: Harvard University Press, 1990), pp. 4–5.

25 Mark Tushnet, 'Critical Legal Studies: A Political History,' *Yale Law Journal* 100 (1991), p. 1518.

26 Mary Joe Frug, 'A Postmodern Feminist Legal Manifesto,' *Harvard Law Review* 105, no. 5 (March 1992), pp. 1045–75.

27 Phyllis Goldfarb, 'From the Worlds of "Others": Minority and Feminist Responses to Critical Legal Studies,' *New England Law Review* 26, no. 3 (special issue dedicated to Mary Joe Frug), p. 685. This article, from which the Tushnet quotation above was taken, gives an excellent overview of the debates.

28 See Patricia Williams, *The Alchemy of Race and Rights* (Cambridge, Mass.: Harvard University Press, 1991).

29 This statement occurs at the end of the essay cited above ('Autobiography as De-Facement') p. 81.

30 Ruth Colker, 'The Example of Lesbians: A Posthumous Reply to Professor Mary Joe Frug,' *Harvard Law Review* 105, no. 5 (March 1992), p. 1084.

31 *Harvard Law Review* 105, no. 5, p. 1045.

32 David Marc Gross, 'A Harvard Killing,' *Mirabella*, October 1992, p. 104.

33 *Harvard Law Revue* 105, no. 61/2 (April 1992), p. 14.

34 Ibid., p. 16.

35 This, of course, only betrays the editors' ignorance. See, e.g., Arthur J. Jacobson, 'The Idolatry of Rules: Writing Law According to Moses, with Reference to Other Jurisprudences,' in Drucilla Cornell, Michel Rosenfeld, and David Gray Carlson, *Deconstruction and the Possibility of Justice* (New York and London: Routledge, 1992), 95–151, as well as the recent works of Mieke Bal.

36 *Harvard Law Revue* 105, no. 61/2 (April 1992), p. 16.

37 Ibid., p. 15.

38 Ibid., p. 18.

39 Alan Dershowitz, 'Law Review Parody a Free-Speech Issue,' *Boston Herald*, 23 April 1992, p. 47.

Women and Allegory

The representation of the allegorical text as a veiled or clothed woman and the concomitant representation of various literary acts – reading, translating, glossing, creating a literary tradition – as masculine acts performed on this feminine body recur across narratives. . . . Chaucer's literary concerns may sound quite modern in this book, but I would prefer to say that our present-day critical concerns turn out to be quite medieval.

Dinshaw, *Chaucer's Sexual Poetics*

1 IS THEORY A WOMAN?

When I was first invited to participate in the Bucknell Lectures in Literary Theory, I was sent several of the books that had previously been published in this series. What immediately piqued my curiosity was what appeared to be the series' logo: the image of a woman floating on a cloud. I would like to begin this lecture on women and allegory by analyzing the significance of this floating signifier.

When I arrived at Bucknell University to deliver my two lectures, I was struck anew by the trademark image the moment I saw the posters announcing my lectures. The enlarged image on the lecture poster must have

struck the Bucknell campus as odd even when the lecturer was Frank Kermode, but when the lecturer is female, it is hard to avoid seeing the image as some sort
of a portrait. Why has this image been chosen as the
series logo, not to say, mascot?

The title of the painting, revealed on the back covers
of the books but not on the posters, is *Theory*, painted
in 1779 by Sir Joshua Reynolds for the ceiling of the
library of the Royal Academy of Art, of which he was
president. One of the organizers of the Bucknell series,
Michael Payne, had seen a postcard of the painting in
the gift shop of the Royal Academy of Art in London
and had snapped it up as a rare instance of a pictorial
representation of theory. Theory, indeed, is often conceived as the very *other* of the image: conceptual rather
than sensual, abstract rather than concrete – despite the
etymology that Wlad Godzich recalls in his introduction
to Paul de Man's *The Resistance to Theory*. 'Theory,'
writes Godzich, 'comes from the Greek verb *theorein*, to
look at, to contemplate, to survey.'[1] The Reynolds painting is unusual in that it offers an embodiment for theory.
In my earlier discussion of the personification of 'deconstruction' implicit in my use of the title *The Wake of
Deconstruction*, I asked, 'What does it mean to treat a
theory as an animate being?' Here, I would like to pursue
that question by asking, What does it mean to personify
theory as a *woman*?

In the list of binary oppositions mentioned above –
conceptual versus sensual, abstract versus concrete – the
gender stereotype that should follow would make theory
male. Godzich's description of the Greek role of theorist
certainly suggests as much:

> The act of looking at, of surveying, designated by *theore-
> in* does not designate a private act carried out by a
> cogitating philosopher but a very public one with im-
> portant social consequences. The Greeks designated

certain individuals, chosen on the basis of their probity
and their general standing in the polity, to act as legates
on certain formal occasions in other city states or in
matters of considerable political importance. These individuals bore the title of *theoros*, and collectively con-
stituted a *theoria*. . . . They were summoned on special
occasions to attest the occurrence of some event, to
witness its happenstance, and to then verbally certify its
having taken place. . . . To be sure, other individuals in
the city could see and tell, but their telling was no more
than a *claim* that they had seen something, and it needed
some authority to adjudicate the validity of such a claim.
. . . The individual citizen, indeed even women, slaves,
and children, were capable of . . . perception, but these
perceptions had no social standing.[2]

Theory, then, from the beginning, has to do with the
public sphere, with *publicly* authorized – state-authorized
– witnesses; women and slaves may have perceptions,
but they have no standing, no theory.

But theory in Reynolds's painting is not just a woman,
she is an allegory. It is as allegory that women have most
often been admitted into public art. I think here of Paul
de Man's remarks in 'The Epistemology of Metaphor'
about John Locke's comments about eloquence. Locke,
defending the philosophical authority of literal language
against the abuses of figure, nonetheless conceded that
'Eloquence, like the fair sex, has too prevailing beauties
in it to suffer itself ever to be spoken against.' De Man
comments:

Nothing could be more eloquent than this denunciation
of eloquence. It is clear that rhetoric is something one
can decorously indulge in as long as one knows where it
belongs. Like a woman, which it resembles ('like the fair
sex'), it is a fine thing as long as it is kept in its proper
place. Out of place, among the serious affairs of men ('if
we would speak of things as they are'), it is a disruptive
scandal, – like the appearance of a real woman in a

gentleman's club where it would only be tolerated as a picture, preferably naked (like the image of Truth), framed and hung on the wall.[3]

The way in which this quotation brings rhetoric and gender together with the public/private opposition is interesting. Woman is fine in her proper place (in private), but among the 'serious affairs of men' (in public) a 'real' woman is 'a disruptive scandal.' Woman will only be tolerated as an image. But is a men's club the public sphere? Or rather, is the public sphere a men's club? Certainly recent debates about admitting women as members to such clubs would suggest a crisis of the superimposition of the public/private distinction upon the male/female distinction. The attempt to rename 'all-male' clubs as 'private' only attests to the crisis. Another thing to note about the de Man quotation is that its attempts to tell an allegory of rhetoric get out of hand. The real woman in the men's club is supposed to be a figure for the scandal of rhetoric within philosophical discourse. When she is replaced by a *figure* – the picture on the wall – she is no longer a figure for the real scandal of figure. This energy to contain and reduce the scandal is enacted by de Man's own language in the passage. By arranging the grammar in such a way as to appear to refer to the woman as 'it' ('like the appearance of a real woman in a gentleman's club where *it* would only be tolerated as a picture'), de Man's language prematurely contains the scandal even as he ironizes the act of containing it. In order for de Man to have made his point about the scandal of rhetoric, he would have had to keep the woman real. While ironizing the sexism of the philosophical tradition, de Man's text thus only perpetuates it.

But back to the painting. What is Reynolds's painting saying about theory? The woman is seated on a cloud. Is this Cloud 9? Is Theory dead? The woman is holding a scroll at which she is not looking; she faces away from the clouds that support her elbow and knee and spreads her legs. Does Theory then equal not reading, or becoming ungrounded? Or does it have to do with what is or isn't between a woman's legs? But her raised knee seems about to drift coyly back toward the other leg, as if in an attempt at concealment. Is Theory then the impossibility of deciding between concealment and exposure, the truth that is only revealed when veiled? Perhaps. But what is the woman's relation to the text held loosely in her hand? Has she read it? Did she write it? Why is she looking away from it? Is this simply a pose meant to signify 'contemplation'?

What does the scroll say? I could at first make out the words 'Theory' and 'Nature' in large letters on the scroll, but not the intervening words. Even when I went to visit the painting, now housed rather ignominiously in the stacks of the new Royal Academy library (when the Academy moved from its original quarters in Somerset House, the painting was removed from the ceiling and replaced by a copy), I found that it was not really easy to decipher the text, which reads: 'THEORY is the knowledge of what is truly NATURE.' Interesting definition, I thought, and not one that really corresponds to the contemporary sense of the word. Indeed, it could be said that contemporary theory has substituted the word 'culture' for the Enlightenment concept of 'Nature', so that a definition of contemporary theory would more accurately read: 'Theory is the knowledge of what is truly Culture,' Nature being a concept that is now seen as a back- formation constructed differently by each culture to stand in for what is (culturally) *defined* as outside culture.

But back to the painting. What is the relation between the scroll and the woman, or between text and image? Is the scroll functioning as her name tag ('Hello . . . my name is THEORY')? Is the text *equivalent* to the image, both functioning as representations of theory, one in the form of a statement, the other in the form of a personification? Or is the painting a representation of theory as the *incommensurability* of language and image? The more I looked at the painting, the more there seemed to be energy *separating* the woman from the scroll, as though she were dreamily *not* paying attention to it, as though she were dissociating herself from it. Resistance to theory, perhaps? Or perhaps the woman was not really meant to represent Theory at all, but rather Nature, the object to be truly known by Theory, which remains unrepresented since it corresponds not to the image but to the gaze of the beholder. This interpretation, however, seems a bit too overdetermined by familiar patterns of women as Nature and men as observers, of women as objects and men as subjects of the gaze. I decided to turn to the *Discourses* of Sir Joshua Reynolds for possible clarification.

In the texts of the discourses that Reynolds delivered annually or semi-annually to the Academy during his presidency, I could find no female personification of Theory, but plenty of female images of Nature. Here are some examples:

> I cannot help imagining that I see a promising young painter equally vigilant, whether at home or abroad, in the streets or in the fields. . . . He regards all Nature with a view to his profession, and combines her beauties, or corrects her defects.[4]

> The great use of studying our predecessors is to open the mind, to shorten our labor, and to give us the result of selection made by those great minds of what is grand or beautiful in nature, her rich stores are all spread out before us.[5]

> Study nature attentively, but always with those masters in your company; consider them as models which you

are to imitate, and at the same time as rivals with whom you are to contend.[6]

An oedipal pattern emerges from these quotations: the young painter is first alone with Mother Nature, then inducted into the Father's mastery, then becomes a rival with the Father for possession of Nature. Theory is not named, but Reynolds refers to his discourses as a theory of art whose job it is to advise students in the academy as to how to negotiate between the imitation of the masters and the knowledge of nature. The other word Reynolds uses for what he desires to teach is 'taste,' and taste is described in terms reminiscent of the words inscribed on our scroll: 'The beginning, the middle, and the end of every thing that is valuable in taste, is comprised in the knowledge of what is truly nature; for whatever notions are not conformable to those of Nature, or universal opinion, must be considered as more or less capricious.'[7]

As president of the Royal Academy, Reynolds's investment in the question of theory is inextricable from his attempts to justify the very existence of an academy. This need for justification may indeed also underlie the sense of crisis introduced into literary studies by literary theory; that is, the resistance to theory is a resistance to acknowledging that theory is inseparable from the concept of a literary academy, since something has to stand as an answer to the question of what it means to *study* literature. What can an art academy teach a man of genius? This was certainly Blake's withering question in his marginalia to Reynolds. Why can't a genius just go out and paint Nature? Reynolds must justify theory in order to justify the academy while continuing to give the concept of Nature a controlling, if contradictory, authority. The contradiction in Nature's authority is introduced through the seemingly minor qualification in the above quotation of what nature is. Reynolds speaks of notions derived from 'Nature, *or universal opinion*.' He goes on to say that 'Deformity is not nature, but an accidental deviation from her accustomed practice.'[8] That is, Nature is not found, but made, through universal opinion, as an idealization. The painter who would paint from nature would not necessarily be painting Nature: 'Nature herself is not to be too closely copied . . . All the arts receive their perfection from an ideal beauty, superior to what is to be found in individual nature.'[9] If theory is the knowledge of what is truly nature, then it is clear that what nature is, is truly theory.

Where, then, does this leave us in relation to the question of the gender of theory? Let me add another quotation from Sir Joshua:

> When we have had continually before us the great works of art to impregnate our minds with kindred ideas, we are then, and not til then, fit to produce something of the same species.[10]

Who is the woman now? It seems that the student here must take up a woman's place and become impregnated by the ancestor in order to produce art that will perpetuate the species. The press of figuration produces male femininity. Is the woman on the cloud then a man in drag? In a sense, yes; since, as an allegory, the female figure is not a literal representation of a woman as artist or theorist – not a 'real woman' – but rather an enabling figure for the production of male artists. 'Woman' is thus both that which is not, and that without which there cannot be, theory.

I would like to mention quickly two other examples of the appropriation of femininity for the grounding of male authority. The *locus classicus* of the simultaneity of the female as Muse and the male as pregnant is of course Sir Philip Sidney's first sonnet in *Astrophel and Stella*, which describes an enamored man with a writer's block caught between Nature and Study. The sonnet ends:

> Thus, great with child to speak, and helpless in my
>   throes,
> Biting my truant pen, beating myself for spite:
> 'Fool,' said my Muse to me, 'look in thy heart, and
>   write.'

My second example comes from Jacques Derrida's *Memoires for Paul de Man*, from which I quoted earlier. The book begins with an invocation of Mnemosyne, the Muse of Memory, the mother of all the Muses. I am tempted to see the invocation of this female figure in the opening lecture of Derrida's mourning for de Man as some kind of camouflage or relief from the pressures of homosocial desire that inevitably animate the project. In the course of the text, Derrida writes about mourning as follows:

> We can only live this experience in the form of an aporia: the aporia of mourning and of prosopopoeia, where the possible remains impossible. Where *success fails*. And where faithful interiorization bears the other and constitutes him in me (in us), at once living and dead. It makes the other a *part* of us, between us – and then the other no longer quite seems to be the other, because we grieve for him and bear him *in us*, like an unborn child, like a future. And inversely, the *failure succeeds*: an aborted interiorization is at the same time a respect for the other as other, a sort of tender rejection, a movement of renunciation which leaves the other alone, outside, over there, in his death, outside of us.[11]

Which is the proper image of mourning of a man for a man – pregnancy or abortion? Which is the proper response to the otherness of the other?

Derrida's emphasis on the question of the other as other is related to his analysis of Paul de Man's several discussions of the question of allegory, and implicitly to the etymology of the *word* 'allegory': *allos*, 'other'; *agorein*, 'to speak in the open square,' from *agora*, 'the marketplace, the public sphere.' Allegory is speech that is other than open, public, direct. It is hidden, deviant, indirect – but also, I want to emphasize, public. It folds the public onto itself. It names the conflictuality of the public sphere and the necessity of negotiating those conflicts rhetorically. If allegory thus provides a model for discursive struggles in the public sphere, might Paul de Man's theories of allegory shed any light on the types of conflicts I discussed in the earlier sections of this book? I will try to approach this question in the final section, but first I would like to draw upon de Man's theory of allegory to move toward a different reading of Reynolds's *Theory*.

2 ALLEGORY AND READABILITY

In 'The Rhetoric of Temporality,' de Man contests the privilege accorded by many critics to 'symbolic' as opposed to 'allegorical' language in the rhetoric of Romanticism. He describes that privilege in the following terms:

> The supremacy of the symbol, conceived as an expression of unity between the representative and the semantic function of language, becomes a commonplace that underlies literary taste, literary criticism, and literary history.[12]

> Commentators . . . define the romantic image as a relationship between mind and nature, between subject and object.[13]

> The subjectivity of experience is preserved when it is translated into language; the world is then no longer seen as a configuration of entities that designate a plurality of distinct and isolated meanings, but as a configuration of symbols ultimately leading to a total, single,

and universal meaning. This appeal to the infinity of a
totality constitutes the main attraction of the symbol as
opposed to allegory . . . Allegory appears as dryly ra-
tional and dogmatic in its reference to a meaning that it
does not itself constitute, whereas the symbol is founded
on an intimate unity between the image that rises up
before the senses and the supersensory totality that the
image suggests.[14]

The relationship with nature has been superseded by an
intersubjective, interpersonal relationship that, in the
last analysis, is a relationship of the subject toward itself.[15]

De Man sees this metaphorical equivalence between
mind and nature, this immediate readability of nature's
symbolic significance, as a mystification that does *not* in
fact characterize the most lucid moments of Romantic
writing. He takes Rousseau's novel *Julie, ou La Nouvelle
Heloïse* as his proof text. In that novel, Rousseau indeed
depicts moments at which Nature – particularly wild,
turbulent Nature – reflects the state of the characters'
souls. But such immediately readable, instantaneous,
metaphorical passions, whether between mind and nature or between man and woman, are precisely what the
text tries to teach its reader to see as an error and
renounce. The landscape that encodes this superior lu-
cidity is Julie's carefully tended 'English' garden, where
the appearance of naturalness is produced by artifice and
where the sources are literary (from the *Romance of the
Rose* to *Pilgrim's Progress*), not natural. 'It remains
necessary, if there is to be allegory,' writes de Man, 'that
the allegorical sign refer to another sign that precedes
it.'[16] He then concludes:

Whereas the symbol postulates the possibility of an
identity or identification, allegory designates primarily a
distance in relation to its own origin, and, renouncing

the nostalgia and the desire to coincide, it establishes its language in the void of this temporal difference. In so doing, it prevents the self from an illusory identification with the non-self.[17]

'Symbol' is thus a 'temptation,'[18] the temptation of immediate readability, which turns out to be a denial of the structure of representation and of the difference between self and non-self. 'Allegory' is the recognition of the difference between signifier and signified, of the relation between any use of language and its linguistic or cultural past, and of the difference between self and other.

If we look back at Reynolds's *Theory*, we can connect de Man's discussion of symbol and allegory with our discussion of the painting in two ways. Reynolds, a contemporary of Rousseau, was struggling in his *Discourses* with the very same issues of representing Nature. On the one hand, the artist was to depict the beauties of nature 'herself.' On the other hand, the artist was to study the 'masters' and learn the idealizations of 'universal opinion.' Reynolds's language alternates between a 'symbolic' wishing away of the difference and an 'allegorical' recognition of the relation between present and past representations.

But my discussion of *Theory* relates to these questions in another way as well. In seeking to read the painting directly, in trying to decipher its statements about gender and theory *by looking at it*, I have been 'guilty' of attempting to read the painting 'symbolically' rather than 'allegorically.' Can it be taken at 'face' value? How does it relate to its own pictorial past? What is the nature of its readability?

When I was looking through materials in the Witt Library about Reynolds's painting, I came across the reproduction of an engraving of the painting done by J. Grozer in 1785. In the engraving, there were two lines radiating out from Theory's head, making her look like

Ray Walton in 'My Favorite Martian.' (I cite this television reference to demonstrate the inescapability of intertextuality, even the wrong kind.) The description of Reynolds's ceiling painting given by Joseph Baretti in his official guide gives a clue as to the significance of those lines. His description, which places Theory in the context of the four other paintings on the Royal Academy library ceiling, reads as follows:

> The Center-Painting represents the *Theory of the Art* under the form of an elegant and majestick female, seated in the clouds, and looking upwards, as contemplating the Heavens. She holds in one hand the Compass, in the other a Label, on which this sentence is written: THEORY is the Knowledge of what is truly NATURE.[19]

Since the compass is undetectable in the painting as it now stands, where did it go? And where did it come from?

Figure 1   Image of Theory, from Cesare Ripa, *Iconologia or Moral Emblems* (New York: Garland Publishing, 1976), p. 73.

It seems to me fitting that it should have been a missing compass that alerted me to the painting's status as sign referring to a previous sign. One clear ancestor of Reynolds's painting, whatever may have been the intermediary images he may have followed, can be found in an important book of Renaissance allegorical images: Cesare Ripa's *Iconologia*, published in Rome in the early 1600s.[20] Figure 1 shows Ripa's image of Theory. In the 1709 English translation of Ripa, the description of Theory runs as follows:

> A young Woman looking upward; her Hands clasp'd together; a pair of Compasses over her head; nobly clad in Purple; seeming to descend the Stairs.
>
> The colour of her Garment shews that the *Sky* terminates our Sight; her Face, that the Intellect is taken up with *celestial* Things; the Stairs, that Things intelligible have Order, proceeding by *Degrees* from Things near to Things a far off. The Compasses are the most proper Instrument of *Measuring*, which Perpetuate the Name of an Author.[21]

For contrast, Figure 2 shows Ripa's image of Practice, which is described in the following terms:

> Opposite to *Theory*. She is aged; her Head inclin'd; a pair of Compasses in one Hand, and a Rule in the other. She's dress'd in a servile Manner.
>
> Her down Looks denote her regarding only that part we *tread* on, and *abject* Things, as appears by her Robe. Theory does not doat on *Custom*, but relies on the true *Knowledge* of Things. The Compasses denote *Reason*, necessary for the due Conduct of Affairs: the Rule, the *Measure* of Things, establish'd by common Consent.[22]

In the sharp contrast between young and old, up and down, sky and ground, Ripa expresses a clear preference for theory over practice. But in the question of custom and measurement, the same ambiguity arises that

Figure 2   Image of Practice, from Cesare Ripa, *Iconologia or Moral Emblems* (New York: Garland Publishing, 1976), p. 60.

Reynolds attempted to finesse by speaking of 'Nature, or universal opinion.' Is measurement theory or practice? truth or custom? The compasses, themselves double, serve as a double sign.

When I attempted to ask the painting what it was saying about the relation between women and theory, I was acting as though it was Reynolds who had chosen to incarnate theory as female. But if Reynolds was merely repeating an existing emblem, what does it mean to ask about the significance of its gender? Perhaps we should be asking what *Ripa* was saying about women through the femininity of Theory and Practice. A glance through the *Iconologia* will tell us that although Academia, Idleness, Flattery, Agriculture, Authority, and Democracy are female, while Despair, Assistance, Artifice, Credit, and Tax are male, it is not because Ripa is consciously intending to say something about gender.

The genders of the figures are based solely on the genders of the Italian nouns. Their gendered embodiment thus arises out of a *non*-referential, intralinguistic aspect of language.

To read the painting 'symbolically' was to assume that it was what it looked like, that its meaning was readable from its face. To read the painting 'allegorically' was to uncover both the historical ancestors and the linguistic determinations of the image. Even Ripa is not the 'origin,' since he describes his emblems as 'designed by the ancient Egyptians, Greeks, Romans, and modern Italians.' Does this mean that the 'symbolic' reading has no place, that the only non-mystified route to the significance of the painting is through the infinite regress of history and convention, through its relation to 'another sign that precedes it'? Does the fact that Theory is a woman have *no* significance for the role of gender in culture?

3 ALLEGORY AND IDENTITY POLITICS

In 1979, ten years after 'The Rhetoric of Temporality,' de Man returned to allegory and to Rousseau's *Julie* for a further analysis. In the later work, he expands upon the ethical dimension of the novel earlier discussed in terms of 'renunciation.' Here the mystification previously named by 'symbol' is replaced by the fallacy of attempting to find a referential grounding for metaphor, enacted in the passion between Julie and Saint-Preux as the mystified belief in the sameness of their two souls. 'Allegories are always allegories of metaphor,' he writes, 'and, as such, they are always allegories of the impossibility of reading.'[23] When *Julie* substitutes a discourse of renunciation and virtue for the failed metaphor of love, the text attempts to make its epistemology and its morality fit together. But allegory is the story of the impossibility of doing so. The allegorical narrative 'knows' that language can neither be referentially reliable *nor avoid referentiality*, but it needs the authority of referentiality ('truth or falsehood') in order to ground its moral imperatives ('right or wrong'):

> In the allegory of unreadability, the imperatives of truth and falsehood oppose the narrative syntax and manifest themselves at its expense. The concatenation of the categories of truth and falsehood with the values of right and wrong is disrupted, affecting the economy of the narration in decisive ways. We can call this shift in economy *ethical*, since it indeed involves a displacement from *pathos* to *ethos*. Allegories are always ethical, the term ethical designating the structural interference of two distinct value systems. In this sense, ethics has nothing to do with the will (thwarted or free) of a subject, nor *a fortiori*, with a relationship between subjects. The ethical category is imperative (i.e., a category rather than a value) to the extent that it is linguistic and not subjective. Morality is a version of the same language aporia that gave rise to such concepts as 'man' or 'love' or 'self,' and not the cause or the consequence of such concepts.[24]

In other words, given that there is a question about what the concepts 'man,' 'love,' or 'self' actually *name* – that is, whether they denominate an existing entity or *posit* its existence – these terms are already caught up in the question of whether truth and falsehood are themselves constitutive or contractual, denominative or imperative. Allegories would be narratives of the difficulty of getting any of these terms to settle into reliable starting points for the formulation of ethical or moral imperatives. The aporia consists in the fact that, although it is impossible to formulate an ethical or moral imperative *without* concepts like 'man', 'love,' or 'self,' the concepts themselves already raise all the issues that they are being used to formulate and to resolve.

How does all this work in a given *narrative* allegory? Let us look at the opening lines of John Bunyan's *Pilgrim's Progress*:

> As I walked through the wilderness of this world, I lighted on a certain place, where was a den; and I laid me down in that place to sleep: and as I slept I dreamed a dream. I dreamed, and behold I saw a man clothed with rags, standing in a certain place, with his face from his own house, a book in his hand, and a great burden upon his back. I looked, and saw him open the book, and read therein; and as he read, he wept and trembled: and not being able longer to contain, he brake out with a lamentable cry; saying, 'What shall I do?'[25]

This question can stand as the sign of allegory as ethics: the reader in the text asks not 'What does this text mean?' nor even 'How does this text signify?' but rather, 'What shall I do?'

Pilgrim's Progress asks the question 'What shall I do?' in the context of a dream of reading.[26] If allegory is indeed central to deconstructive theory, then deconstruction's 'wake' will have to be recognized as a form of 'sleep.' Nothing in Bunyan's character's demeanor is proof that the text he is reading is, in fact, readable – his tears might be precisely the sign of its unreadability. Where does Bunyan's allegory start? With sleep? with seeing a double? with reading? with walking through the wilderness of this world? with asking 'What shall I do?'

For de Man, the question 'What shall I do?' would stand precisely as the ethical effect of allegory's unreadability, an unreadability produced by the interference of the two incompatible frameworks of which it is composed: reference and judgment. Later in Bunyan's allegory, the question is extended: 'What shall I do *to be saved*?' Does allegory – or ethics – necessarily arise within a horizon of salvation? No less an authority than Rosemond Tuve describes salvation as 'the basic theme of allegory.'[27]

To seek illumination on the question of salvation, I turned to a book by law professor Derrick Bell, the first African-American tenured at Harvard Law School, entitled *And We Are Not Saved*.[28] The book is a reflection on the repeated failures of civil rights movements in the United States – abolition, reconstruction, the civil rights movement of the sixties, affirmative action, and so on – to bring about the racial justice for which they had been undertaken. But Bell's is no ordinary work of legal theory. It is structured around ten chronicles told to the narrator by an allegorical black woman lawyer named Geneva Crenshaw, a person the narrator once knew, who was wounded by racists during the Mississippi summer voter registration drive of 1964 and with whom the narrator had lost touch until she contacted him by e-mail and arranged to meet him and tell him about her travels through time, from the Constitutional Convention of 1787 to the present. After she has finished narrating these chronicles, she again drops out of sight. The narrative opens with the narrator dozing at a civil rights convention and waking up to find himself handed transcripts of those conversations, which he had thought private. Here, once again, we find ourselves waking into allegory through sleep. And, once again, we encounter a female Muse – the equivalent of the dead woman as voice-from-beyond-the-grave – and a second mourning (she has now disappeared again) as the opening into the public sphere.

Shortly after completing this book, Derrick Bell must have read it, understood it, and asked himself 'What shall I do?' What he did was to go on strike against Harvard Law School, promising to return only after they had hired and tenured an African-American woman. As a response to the allegorical strategy of meeting women only in a different rhetorical dimension – the picture of

Truth on the wall of the gentleman's club, the picture of Theory on the ceiling of the Royal Academy of Art – Bell wanted to reveal the rhetorical fold that overdetermined his own creation of the authoritative black woman as dead and allegorical and to produce what de Man had called the 'disruptive scandal' of a real black woman on the faculty of Harvard Law School. More than two years have passed since Bell began his strike, and the Law School has not yet tenured a black woman. But Bell himself has been forced to resign from Harvard for exceeding the two-year limit allowed to tenured professors for leaves of absence.

What I want to suggest is that Bell's use of allegory, on the one hand, and his strike to protest the lack of diversity at Harvard Law School, on the other, are rhetorically inseparable. Identity politics – the politics of representativity, of speaking 'as a,' as Nancy Miller has discussed it[29] – involve the translation of the structure of allegory into the reconstruction of the social text. What could more resemble the cast of characters in Bunyan than the list of participants recommended by an ad hoc group to compose a *Revue* Action Committee to investigate the circumstances and the significance of the misogynist parody of the dead Mary Joe Frug's 'Postmodern Feminist Legal Manifesto':

> The Dean of Students, two female members of the *Law Review*, at least one of whom is also a member of a Minority Group, two representatives from the Law School Council, one representative from the Law School Staff, one representative from each of the following organizations, should they choose to participate: Asian-American Law Students Association; Black Law Students Association; Committee on Gay, Bisexual, and Lesbian Legal Issues; Jewish Law Students Association; La Alianza; Middle Eastern Law Students Association; South Asian Law Students Association; Students for Disability Rights; Women's Law Association; and a faculty member.

This list was circulated by the establishment and in the press as a laughable nightmare of political correctness. That Harvard Law School should be critically read by this jury of its peers seems to have been felt as equivalent to Bunyan's Christian and Faithful facing a jury composed of Mr Blind-Man, Mr No-Good, Mr Malice, Mr Love-Lust, Mr Live-Loose, Mr Heady, Mr High-Mind, Mr Enmity, Mr Liar, Mr Cruelty, Mr Hate Light, and Mr Implacable. To the extent that identity politics presupposes that human beings are personifications of their readable traits, that each person represents synecdochally – and 'symbolically' in de Man's sense – the group to which he or she belongs, the social text would indeed become balkanized and clogged with its own readability. But to see the current operation of identity politics as conforming to this 'symbolic' model of allegory is to miss the ways in which the identities in question are based on 'contractual' rather than 'essential' premises. The committee list cited above is not composed of substantialized adjectives – one black, one Asian, one lesbian, and so forth – but rather of represetatives of already existing political organizations – loci of an ongoing and already existing *self*-critique within the institution. Each time a person chooses to speak 'as a,' he or she is attempting the 'ethical' leap that de Man's later analysis associates with allegory: to combine referentiality (the question of identity) with judgment (the question of social change), to make the true/false distinction line up with the right/wrong distinction. This is what de Man referred to as allegory's 'unreadability.' But such a politics of location and subject position does not dismiss as mere mystification the question of the readability of human beings as signs. Human beings *are* constantly being read – and misread. Just because identities are fictions does not mean that they have not had, and could not have, real historical effects. It is not true, for example, that the gender of Reynolds's *Theory* has had no impact on sexual politics. Just because the image's gender derives from a 'mere' linguistic fiction (the gender of a noun) does not mean that the existence of half-clad, nameless women on the walls and ceilings of public spaces – or on book covers – has not shaped the cultural messages addressed both to women and to men. It is just that the 'cause' of the cultural messages cannot easily be tied to intentions.

The outrage and resistance, the appeals to free speech, on the part of those (mainly but not exclusively white males) who identify with the voice of the institution of law or of the law school is a resistance to *being read* – being read speaking 'as a' rather than simply speaking; being read through a predicate of embodiment, location, interest, and readability, rather than through the disembodied, authorized, official impersonality of the *theoria*. If they see themselves as personifications, it is as personifications of the whole – humanity, reason, law, truth – not personifications within a psychomachia for control of the social text.

But the resistance to being read 'as a' is just as necessary as the acknowledgment of positionality – indeed, that resistance has prompted the struggle against reductive stereotypes in the first place. The challenge is to analyze a history of effects other than by seeking to identify personifiable causes, to recognize that nevertheless the struggle is taking place as much among personifications as among persons, and to intervene to transform the social allegory without either buying into, or dismissing, the temptations of readability. For the necessity of reading and being read is a dream from which we cannot awaken.

NOTES

1 Wlad Godzich, Foreword to Paul de Man, *The Resistance to Theory* (Minneapolis: University of Minnesota Press, 1986), p. xiv.
2 Ibid.

3   Paul de Man, 'The Epistemology of Metaphor,' in *On Metaphor*, ed. Sheldon Sacks (Chicago: University of Chicago Press, 1978), pp. 13–14.

4   Sir Joshua Reynolds, *Discourses*, ed. Edmund Gosse (London: Kegan Paul, Trench, & Co., 1884), p. 29.

5   Ibid., p. 94.

6   Ibid., p. 109.

7   Ibid., p. 119.

8   Ibid.

9   Ibid., p. 32.

10   Ibid., p. 92.

11   Jacques Derrida, *Memoires for Paul de Man* (New York: Columbia University Press, 1986), p. 35.

12   Paul de Man, 'The Rhetoric of Temporality', first published in *Interpretation*, ed. Charles Singleton (Baltimore: Johns Hopkins University Press, 1969); reprinted in Paul de Man, *Blindness and Insight*, 2 edn., (Minneapclis: University of Minnesota Press, 1983). Quotations are from the latter; here p. 189.

13   Ibid., p. 193.

14   Ibid., pp. 188–9.

15   Ibid., p. 196.

16   Ibid., p. 207.

17   Ibid.

18   Ibid., p. 205.

19   Quoted in *Reynolds*, ed. Nicholas Penny (catalogue published by the Royal Academy of Arts, London, 1986), p. 284. Interestingly, among the four allegorical paintings in the four corners of the ceiling is a painting of Nature described as 'a lady nursing one child and simultaneously exhibiting herself to infant artists.' The other three paintings are of History, Allegory, and Fable. Nature and History present a woman surrounded by infants; Allegory and Fable present infants surrounded by emblems (Allegory) and monsters (Fable).

20   I would like to thank Stephen Orgel for leading me to the book that saved me from my ignorance: *The Renaissance Imagination: Essays and Lectures by D. J. Gordon*, collected and edited by Stephen Orgel (Berkeley: University of California Press, 1975).

21 Cesare Ripa, *Iconologia or Moral Emblems* (New York: Garland Publishing, 1976), p. 74.
22 Ibid., p. 61.
23 Paul de Man, *Allegories of Reading* (New Haven, Conn.: Yale University Press, 1979), p. 205.
24 Ibid., p. 206.
25 John Bunyan, *The Pilgrim's Progress* (Harmondsworth: Penguin, 1965), p. 39.
26 It should be noted that Bunyan wrote not one but two *Pilgrim's Progresses*, the first about a man, Christian, the second about his wife, Christiana, and their four children, all sons. In Christiana's case, there is also an act of sleeping and reading, but what she reads is a parchment containing the record of her sins, primary among which is her sin against her husband for not accompanying him on his journey. Thus, while Christian sets off for sin alone, Christiana is persuaded to go for sin against her husband.
27 Rosemond Tuve, *Allegorical Imagery* (Princeton, N.J.: Princeton University Press, 1966), p. 49.
28 Derrick Bell, *And We Are Not Saved* (New York: Basic Books, 1987).
29 Nancy K. Miller, *Getting Personal* (New York: Routledge, 1991).

An Interview with Barbara Johnson

Conducted by Michael Payne and Harold Schweizer

PAYNE About the time we conceived of this Mellon Project, Walter Jackson Bate published his essay, 'The Crisis in English Studies.' Reading that essay from here, I couldn't help but wonder if it represented a polar opposition, at Harvard, to all the work in theory at Yale, which was being so widely publicized. Could you give a little institutional history here? What was the stance towards theory at Harvard when you began to teach there?

JOHNSON Harvard is not a monolith and really never has been. In the English department, Walter Jackson Bate did have a dominant voice that seemed to stand for Harvard, as did Harry Levin in comparative literature. I don't want to underestimate the degree to which such voices did seem to represent the views of the institution, but there were also always other professors whose work was different or whose students learned different things, although it is only fairly recently and precariously that theory, feminism, Marxism, Afro-American literature, gay studies, and interdisciplinary studies have become part of the Harvard English department offerings. One of the interesting crossovers is that while Bate's essay 'The Crisis in English Studies' seemed to represent Harvard as standing for the value of traditional 'spirit of the age' literary history as Bate knew it – and Yale or theory as standing for an attack on meaning or an attack on literary monuments – in fact, one of the origins of American deconstruction, as Paul de Man pointed out in his response to Bate, was Reuben Brower at Harvard, a colleague of Bate's whose teaching fellow de Man was, as was, I think, Neil Hertz. So de Man was in a way a Harvard product. Institutions, I think, are seldom as monolithic as they appear from a distance, although the wall they can erect against unwanted ideas can seem quite impenetrable. The impact of places like Harvard, Yale, Duke, and so on is based on a fictional identity which corresponds only loosely to the facts and the actual curriculum, since it represses internal struggles and differences. Nevertheless, belief in that fictional identity gives it a certain historical reality through its effects. When I first got to Harvard, I was in the French department, which, under the leadership of Jules Brody, had been undergoing a major change in personnel because of retirements and various other things. And so, the Harvard that I entered already included Susan Suleiman and Alice Jardine. Therefore I didn't go from Yale directly to the Harvard English department, which probably preserved some years of my life. But at the moment, the Harvard English department has become very much more diverse and very much more in tune with contemporary developments in criticism.

PAYNE Do you think it was only in the press that a sense of an institutional identity at Yale was created, or do you think that the institution where theorists practice affects in some significant way the formation of their theoretical work?

JOHNSON If you're asking whether theory would have developed in the same way if it had sprung up elsewhere, I don't know whether there is any way of knowing that. Certainly it *was* springing up in different ways in different places. Yale got more credit – and blame – for it than was accurate. There was certainly resistance to theory *within* Yale. Nevertheless, there was a group of congenial and productive male scholars in their late 40s or so – Paul de Man, Geoffrey Hartman, Hillis Miller, and, to some extent, Harold Bloom (Bloom was probably younger, but he didn't seem so) – who were all working on Romanticism and rhetoric and who found each other's work interesting. Also, Yale was the place that first invited Derrida for extended visits. And at the same time probably the fact that Yale was also a location for New Critics made the theoretical developments in the seventies take on the particular cast that they took, that there seemed to be more of an affiliation between American deconstruction and New Criticism because of the fact that New Criticism and Deconstruction were both developed by major people at Yale.

PAYNE My impression is that, in Britain especially, literary theory is entering universities in a sense from the bottom up rather than from the top down. Not just that Oxford and Cambridge have been somewhat resistant to work in theory but also that people without jobs or people who are teaching in the open university are writing significant books and articles on theory. Now, it would seem in the States that the situation is the opposite, that one or several major institutions with tremendous reputations were places where the most important early theory was taking shape in the sixties and seventies. First, is that distinction accurate, and is it significant, and, secondly, has it been good for the spread of theoretical work that there is a sense of intellectual and institutional prestige attached to it in America?

JOHNSON First, it depends on what you mean by theory. Feminist theory, for example, was not, or not only, developed from the top down, and still isn't, although it has been very much affected by debates with other forms of theory. What is commonly referred to in the United States as 'theory' is a combination of structuralism, deconstruction, psychoanalysis, philosophy, poetics, and cultural materialism – but often 'theory' refers primarily to deconstruction. Theory in the United States is a more conservative, canonical, academic enterprise than the kind of theory coming from the margins of the academy in Britain, where the connections to politics are closer, and where there are more underemployed intellectuals around. I think, probably, in the United States, the combination of an interest in new things and an interest in European intellectuals combine to make the prestigious universities more receptive to theory than in England, where the propagation of a kind of legacy that is English and that is not foreign and not new is more entrenched in the way the university functions. That doesn't mean that there isn't, in the United States, a 'legacy' mentality, where the tradition is transmitted from one venerable man to his 'sons,' but because of the many shifts in populations and the increasing diversity of the student body it is not clear exactly what the filiations are. And the United States, after all, was *founded* in opposition to the European tradition of inherited privilege. When the Declaration of Independence states that governments derive their powers from the consent of the governed, this is a *theoretical* statement. When had it ever been true? Of course, there is also, in the United States, a suspicion of theory, that someone too articulate is likely to be a con man or that someone who uses big words is likely not to be reliable. It is also true that culture is seen sometimes as still emanating from Europe, continuing the American inferiority complex that Emerson lamented. And so, people like René Wellek and de Man and Derrida, people trained in the European philosophical tradition and in multiple languages, have a certain appeal, because such cosmopolitan culture is rarer among native-born Americans.

SCHWEIZER In the introduction to *A World of Difference*, you express your dissatisfaction with linguistic universality and deconstructive allegory, and you promise to attempt to transfer the analysis of difference to the real world. But in order for that promise to be fulfilled, we must pass through a world of words, or, if I may say, up and down an aesthetic ivory tower, or to a realm which you call in one chapter 'the unbypassable site of the penultimate.' Your political ambition, as well as the notion of an ultimate value beyond the penultimate, implies that the tower is not standing firmly and that the textual predicament is insufficiently real if there is beyond it a real world. There seemed to be larger issues of social justice and political relevance that make fierce demands on you. How would you respond to such a reading of your book as a document of some sort of aesthetic crisis?

JOHNSON Do you mean to imply that the real world isn't a world of words?

SCHWEIZER To propose a transfer from linguistic universality to the real world would certainly imply the separability of these two realms.

JOHNSON It's not that language and the world are separate, but that analyzing a literary representation of a real-world issue is not the same thing as facing that issue and having to do something about it in a particular context. Analysis and action are not necessarily separable, but they may obey different temporalities. I think that the real world, the so-called real world, *is* something that can be studied through language. What I had in mind there had a lot to do with the particular object I was using to think about difference, allegorically that is, the opposition between prose and poetry. Baudelaire's prose poems were rewritings of his verse poems that revealed the exclusionary, erasing gestures which lyric poetry had used to create an impression of self-sufficiency. Mallarmé's prose poems went on to explore the way prose usually represses spacing, which poetry foregrounds. The analysis of Baudelaire and Mallarmé through the difference between poetry and prose generated a whole logic of difference and of resistance and of repression of difference and so forth that seemed to have implications that might also be present in oppositions that had more of an impact on the way people live. And so on one level a transfer occurred by saying, what if the same logic that I found in the relation between prose and poetry can be found in the relation between male and female or between black and white or between deconstruction and tradition. That there is a logic here of binary oppositions, how they get set up, how their dynamics work, how they enable certain things to become perceptible as meaningful and other things to become marginalized as invisible. And so by taking texts that would raise questions other than those that I had studied of purely, let us say, the nature of poetry, I might talk about the nature of racial difference or sexual difference in similar terms. That wouldn't necessarily mean that I was describing social reality more accurately or at all, but it would mean that what I thought I had learned from talking about prose and poetry might make me see something about social difference that was present in the way social difference is constructed. And so, another way the transfer might occur is to say certain political problems are based on rhetorical structures or are thoroughly shaped and overdetermined by rhetorical structures. In the case of the essay I wrote, 'Apostrophe, Animation, and Abortion,' it seemed as if apostrophe

and the attendant personification were inseparable from
the way in which 'person' was discussed in legal texts
and the way in which the investment in the unborn was
structured like apostrophe where a tremendous seduc-
tion is set up because the status of the other, even though
in some purely biological sense 'real,' is both so imagin-
ary and somehow all the more real because of its pro-
jected nature.

SCHWEIZER So instead of an aesthetic crisis you
would say these aesthetic and textual concerns are then
perhaps in surprising ways applicable to the political
situation.

JOHNSON Yes. For example, if you have the president of the United States speaking primarily in three-
word sentences, you could say that our form of
government is affected by the grammatical choices made
by the person who seems to be speaking for the understanding that is to be promoted. And so, if the sound
bite is a grammatical form of common understanding or
of government in this country, that limits the kinds of
things that can be said or understood. If eloquence is no
longer associated with government, where it had been in
the past associated with politics, – just as suspect as the
three-word sentence perhaps – there has got to be a
difference between governing with the 'Read my lips'
style and governing with the 'Four score and seven years
ago' style.

SCHWEIZER You have consistenly drawn attention
to the way such rhetoric can be deconstructed. Your own
critical practice results frequently in the claim that textual problems are in the final analysis undecidable. I ask
myself if deconstruction and undecidability are not, as
Terry Eagleton once put it, the unmistakable sign of the
privilege of those who can afford not to know. Now I

think, for example, of abortion, or even of pregnancy, as a situation where such a privilege is radically called into question.

JOHNSON   You mean, if the person is or isn't allowed to have an abortion, the question of the undecidability of the referent is not helpful?

SCHWEIZER   You can't expect that that decision is easily recognizable as a good decision or that you choose between good and evil.

JOHNSON   That may be precisely the nature of decision: you are forced to make one, and you can't give an absolute rationale for it, but whatever you do *is* a decision. But I don't think that all thinking has to take place with the immediate present decision as the direct horizon. I think that if it were true that the only people who are thinking about a problem are the people who must make a decision and whose life is changed by the decision that is made, then certain questions that are relevant would always be cast into the background. That is, certain things that would take more time or certain things that wouldn't give an immediate answer would simply not be dealt with because there would be no time. But there has always been, and I think there should be, the possibility of thinking about the ways in which questions are grounded, that looks at the connection between the point of urgency and all the ways in which that point of urgency takes the form that it takes. If you have to make a decision, the decision presents itself to you in a particular form, but how did that particular form get created? 'Choice' should not only occur on existing terms; there should be choice about what those terms are. It may be that by investigating *that*, decisions might come to people in a different way and that there is something oppressive about having to take the terms of every decision as they come. But to return to the question of undecidability, Terry Eagleton says things like 'Undecidability won't tell us what to do about the boat people.' But just saying *that* won't either. Theoretical statements, whether about decision or about undecidability, are all equally detached from any *particular* intervention.

SCHWEIZER This is a question somewhat beyond these concerns: in the introduction to *The Critical Difference* you state that 'Literature is the discourse most preoccupied with the unknown.' Then you go on to claim that 'The unknown is not what lies beyond the limits of knowledge, some unreachable, sacred, ineffable point towards which we vainly yearn.' My question is, How do you know *that*? Why must the unknown be merely a matter of world enough and time? In my view the unknown would then not be totally unknown, and literature would then not be radically mysterious.

JOHNSON I think it's easy to conceptualize an unknown that lies beyond the known. In other words, every system of knowledge generates a sense of its own limits, and it therefore paints what lies beyond in its own colors even if it is defined as unknown. But what the system of knowledge may not see as unknown is the thing it is blind to in its very construction. So I wouldn't say that I absolutely think that there is no such thing as an unknown that lies beyond where knowledge can reach, but that that model for the unknown is not surprising; whereas the model of the unknown that says the unknown is right here in the very center of the known and is, in some ways, that which enables a sense of knowing to occur, *is* always a surprise. And I think that literature – and literature is very various, and this certainly doesn't describe all literature – but to me, literature is about that. Of course, when I was talking about literature in that statement it was derived from my reading of people like Mallarmé or Flaubert or other nineteenth-century, post-realist writers. Literature in that context was part of the crisis of transcendence, where the beautiful lie was no longer going to ground the enterprise of seeking meaning, but the medium itself became a site of crisis, language itself became, representation itself became a site of crisis, and the fact that it makes invisible while it makes visible came to be an object of interest.

PAYNE Although there's been some very important and very powerful work done by feminists who are also practitioners of deconstruction, Cynthia Chase and Gayatri Spivak and Peggy Kamuf and Toril Moi, yet the suspicion of other feminists about the use of deconstruction seems a suspicion that has a greater intensity to it than perhaps other forms of skepticism. Is that impression accurate? Is there a particular thorniness or prickliness about deconstruction as it enters into a feminist politics?

JOHNSON It would be disabling to say that since there is no such thing as identity, nothing can be done in the name of women. But if you can show that injustice to women has been, and is being, done in the name precisely of that false concept of identity, then deconstructing identity can be liberating. You spoke of skepticism, but you didn't describe the type of skepticism most likely to motivate feminism: skepticism toward the authority of existing cultural arrangements, toward the supposed 'universality' or 'impartiality' of existing 'truths.' But I think that the necessary and productive debates within feminism about the value of deconstruction connect back to the question of speed. If the vocabulary of theory is seen as a perpetuation of the authority of a certain male philosophical tradition, then it would seem to be obvious that the tool being used, even if being used in a sense of changing the institution or changing the way women are socialized or whatever it is, still the tool itself seems to confirm the superiority of a way of thinking that is derived from the very phallocentric tradition, even if critical of it, still part of it, very much part of it, that is being contested. So that if you take deconstruction as a critique of the Western tradition from within it, that may be what the Western tradition has always been. And there, the question of whether there is a place to stand outside that tradition, outside the vocabulary and the intellectual habits of that which has clearly been generating effects that feminists want to change, is a real question. My sense, and the reason I find theory valuable, is that there is not really an outside to the discourse, that we are all in it and that some of the discourses that would like to oppose dominant discourse from the outside don't recognize the ways in which their formulations of the issues are drawing massively on concepts that themselves are central to the tradition. So there are two questions. One is, How can you effect social change? You don't need to have a perfectly coherent theory to do so; you don't need to have a particularly sophisticated theory to do so. It may be helpful not to. But if intellectual patterns have any determining effect on the way people live, and I think they do, then working on how the reflexes of thinking are inculcated might have an impact. It might not have a very obvious or direct one, but what has happened in the academy in the past ten or twenty years seems to indicate that all these ways of questioning the authority of the tradition have worked together, that the changes would not have occurred in the way that they have if there hadn't been all the space of disagreement among theorists and political activists and essentialists and constructivists and deconstructivists, that somehow all these ways of trying to introduce intellectual space, as well as simply institutional space, for an opening of the canon or of perspectives *have* changed things. I think these things have really complemented each other even if, or most likely *because*, they were often in conflict.

PAYNE   Some of the earliest sustained suspicions that deconstruction is politically disabling were focused particularly on the work of Paul de Man. People who knew Paul de Man and who speak about their relationship with him suggest that there was something really quite special about that relationship. Now, there have been other great theorists in recent times, such as Northrop Frye, who has had tremendous influence, but that influence did not seem quite so charged on the personal level while he was alive or now that he has recently died. Can you describe what there was about Paul de Man that had this extraordinarily powerful effect on so many people? Is it possible to describe?

JOHNSON   Paul de Man was a very unusual person. The sheer pleasure of encountering his intelligence surely explains a good part of the effect he had on people. But also, he didn't seem to care about the petty narcissisms of the profession; he didn't say things in order to sound smart, he didn't seem jealous or competitive (even though he could be quite dismissive). Now, perhaps his lack of petty narcissism was related to the fact that he had bigger fish to keep from frying. But his investment in his work seemed totally genuine. He seemed to be working and writing and thinking *because it mattered*. I think he was empowering to a lot of students and colleagues. At the time of his death I think he was directing twenty-seven Ph.D. dissertations, and he read people's chapters fairly promptly. He held office hours longer than anyone else I've ever known and would have hour-long conversations with students who weren't working with him, just people who wanted to come and talk with him, and they would go out of that conversation saying to themselves, 'I'm really interested in something and it is interesting, I'm going to pursue it. I can do it.' It seemed to me that an awful lot of people felt that he had that effect on them. It was a very noninterventionist way of listening to people talk about their work that nevertheless made their project become theirs as they talked. And I think that's probably the most important thing that he gave, that people felt that they were better able, that it was meaningful for them to continue their project, and that they were capable of doing something interesting.

PAYNE   Your most recent collection of essays, *A World of Difference*, is, in a sense, haunted by de Man, or, at least, one way of reading it is that it is haunted by him. Not just the preface but particularly the essays in the first part of the book. I'm not even sure just how to ask this question, because it's a question that is now so contaminated by public and journalistic attempts to answer it. How have the revelations about de Man's journalistic work led you to rethink his role as a teacher?

JOHNSON   For me the revelations were a great shock. I really felt that the person that I had admired and respected was a different person from the one he had to be now that his whole life became visible, that he was, at least, a much more complex person. It always seemed as if he was complex, but one had no access to the complexity because he said so little about himself or was so little interested in representing himself to anybody – he was more like a kind of backboard or mirror. The revelations made me feel that a lot of the idealization people had felt towards him was based on the blank that he was projecting or he was. So that didn't give me a sense of great confidence in my own curiosity about going further to know him. I mean, I was content to know the person that I thought he was and who was very enabling to me, and his work itself was something I read with interest, and it helped me to think about literature in new ways. And I think that what he could give had more to do with the kinds of questions he asked and the way the text came to respond to him than with what might be called the quotable conclusion of any essay. That is, anyone can write a sentence that says, you can always excuse any guilt because you can never tell whether you are talking about the story that you are telling or about the thing that happened. That's been quoted so many times as a proof that, in fact, de Man was elaborating a theory to make it unnecessary to face guilt. But it isn't clear whether he is lamenting or celebrating the fact that excuses can work. But it is not in sentences like that where the real inspiration of his work lies, I think, because that's of the order of an extension, a provocative hyperbole, or a conclusion drawn from a certain kind of textual work, or a certain kind of encounter with a text that could lead to other conclusions. It was the way he got the text to connect with major questions and to look at an improbable moment like an anacoluthon in Rousseau's *Confessions* and say, here Rousseau is going off in one direction, and then suddenly, grammatically, he drops to another level, giving both a psychological explanation and attributing his action to chance. What does this discrepancy mean? And de Man gets the whole reading out of that. It's the capacity to find those moments where the text does something that will open it up to a new set of questions that was what he could teach. The conclusions were the generalizations that he drew and wouldn't themselves have had the impact if they hadn't been accompanied by that unusual capacity to work a text.

PAYNE The revelations about the early writings, in a sense, have filled a need on the part of those who have been positioning themselves to attack in a wholesale way deconstruction and theory. First of all, why do you think there's such a passion to denounce theory, and why focus that denunciation on de Man?

JOHNSON   Well, part of it comes from confusing undecidability with meaninglessness. If the academy is founded on a sense of meaningfulness and if the possibility of grounding the meaning is what is at issue, then any suggestion that, in fact, analysis will not come to rest but will leave us still with unresolved questions sounds like a withdrawal from the possibility of meaning. And so, on a very crude level, I think, it's a way of trying to protect the authority of statements of meaning from further inquiry. Not that statements of undecidability don't have their own authority, and so there is certainly a considerable amount of simple rivalry involved in the quite necessary desire to contest anything that looks like an absolute conclusion.

PAYNE   Have the journalistic accounts of de Man's past and of his influence on American intellectual life forced people to write explanations or apologies in such a way that the apologies themselves are a result of manipulation?

JOHNSON   Well, in some ways, the difficulty is that the unambiguousness of the attacks are partly attacks on ambiguity or undecidability as a content, and it's very hard to answer an unambiguous attack on ambiguity with ambiguity, or to answer an attack based on no reading with a response based on reading. This is what Derrida tried to do, but it is read, and can't help but be read, as a defense of de Man and as a reading that says, "Ha, ha, I can read better than anybody else and here's how I can open up the text to make it less sure exactly what it means, and therefore de Man can't be proven guilty." But the fact that some people see Derrida as similar to Holocaust deniers is a real violation of Derrida's purpose. It is *because* Derrida takes the reality of the Holocaust seriously that he does not think it is simple to isolate the evil. That is, there is a genuine question about exactly what drawing a boundary around the evil and labeling everything within it evil and everything outside it OK means. All the participants in the debate seem to be wanting to draw that line and say, "Let us remain in the good, let us disavow the evil, let us go on from the Second World War into a world where no such recurrence can be possible." Everybody seems to be acting as if all it would take would be to identify every instance of evil, cast shame upon it, and then we'd be safe. But I think that that's not true. We're all talking about ourselves when we talk about this, and I mean both the attackers and the seeming defenders, when we talk about how to judge de Man. And we're talking about judgment and what it is today in the wake of a world-conquering system that was based on so many certainties that themselves are so hard in some ways to extricate from other aspects of the Western tradition – things like nationalism, identity, evolutionary continuity, organicism. As a monstrosity in the history of European civilization, Nazism is both unique and not unique enough. This is what Derrida has been working on, more with Heidegger probably than with de Man, partly because de Man's early writings are much less important and interesting for intellectual history than what Heidegger wrote. But the quite understandable gesture of simply dissociating oneself from anything that is tainted is something Derrida had decided not to simply enact, but rather to *read* the taint, to say, if there is no way of telling the intellectual history of Europe without being tainted, then it doesn't mean we can't make judgments, and he does make judgments in his essay on de Man. But it does mean that we can never be sure we are external to the thing we are judging.

PAYNE   Is it possible to distinguish American deconstruction, say, centered on de Man and his legacy, from
European deconstruction? Is there a point of departure
of one from the other?

JOHNSON   There is a big difference in style between
Derrida and de Man. De Man writes fairly straightforward grammatical sentences (even though he makes interesting grammatical errors) and has much more of a
traditional tone and style of argument; whereas Derrida
has more than one kind of style, but the style itself is
part of the transformation that he is trying to make
perceptible in thinking. Also, Derrida is much more interested in going through the whole philosophical tradition than in reading literature as the main object of his
interest. I think de Man was really interested in literature
first.

PAYNE   Isn't this what would help to explain something
of the difference in the importance of Heidegger for them?

JOHNSON   True, Derrida's interest in Heidegger is
more centrally philosophical; de Man's, more literary.

SCHWEIZER   It seems to me that your work is entire-
ly devoted to not arriving at conclusions, or not arriving
too early. In one of the chapters in *A World of Difference*,
you seem to regret Hurston's conclusive closing gesture
at the end of *Their Eyes were Watching God*. Since you
choose to write in the genre of the essay, you would seem
to have chosen a genre which is opposed to totalization.
Is this a conscious political choice to respond, in a sense,
to those who would too quickly bring down the axe?

JOHNSON   I don't know if it's conscious. I think it is
stylistic – that is, that I'm really more interested in the
way the question is set up and in how the text or texts

develop it as a question than I am in arriving at something with which I agree or disagree or with which other people might agree or disagree. What I didn't like too much about the Hurston ending, or what I felt was reductive, was that there were a lot of unresolved questions at the end of that novel which this ending made go away without at all resolving or without keeping them as questions. Janie has no visible means of support except the money left to her by the second husband, yet he is simply disavowed by the idealization of the third. It is not clear what she will do, it's not clear what kind of life is available or will be interesting to her, and she seems to glorify the moment of nostalgic self-containment as if that could be a way of life. The novel itself has cast some doubts on the perfection or long-term viability of the relationship with Tea Cake, but the novel forgets these, now that he is dead, and acts as though he were ideal.

SCHWEIZER   But why can't we allow ourselves these moments?

JOHNSON   Oh, I don't say we can't allow ourselves. I think it's probably inevitable that we come to rest somewhere and that that's a necessary moment. I just don't find it as interesting.

SCHWEIZER   It's, of course, not always easy to remember when we rest in an illusion that it is an illusion, and the dangerous thing is to think that it is not. But one of the things that seems to me lacking in the desire to keep things open is that that seems to go along with a certain negativity towards illusion and towards the fiction of closure.

JOHNSON   I think that it's not true that it would always be healthy to see illusion as illusion. When Franz

Fanon is talking about what Sartre had to say about Negritude as a mere negative moment in a dialectic, Fanon says that Negritude could not have made the difference that it has made without our believing in it, however much later we might see that, in fact, it was an idealization. But the historical difference that the Negritude movement made could not have been made if it had been a consciously demystified illusion at the time. And I think that it's true that in order for certain things to happen, sites have to be occupied blindly or out of a passion for justice. I wouldn't necessarily say that the ending of *Their Eyes Were Watching God* is an example of that, but it might be, or it might be that you could say, What's the difference between the main character in *The Awakening* swimming off into the sea probably to die and the main character in *Their Eyes Were Watching God* pulling the world in around her and saying, this is peace? There is a great difference in affect, but they both allow you to keep the questions the novels have raised and still give you an ending. And I think in a way that what you say implies that it would not have necessarily been more productive for theory in this country for everyone to have encountered a demystified de Man, that perhaps the idealized de Man that we did encounter as a teacher enabled things that the fallen de Man would not necessarily have been able to enable. And perhaps the most intellectually productive thing of all, even though painful, is to have had both and be forced to come to terms with both.

SCHWEIZER Speaking about de Man, it seems strange that all of you who had known him so well would speak of such a shock. Of course, on a personal level that is true, but, on the other hand, your insistence on a difference within would have had to prepare you for greater complexity, for the difference being more dramatic than you . . .

JOHNSON   I can't say that it is a completely negative shock because it is a perfect illustration of how you can think you know something and not know what you don't know until what you don't know comes up and hits you in the face. And at the same time it is also a challenge. It's an exegetical challenge and a moral challenge and a historical challenge to say what really can be made of all this, and not from the outside but rather from the inside. There's no way to just leap to the outside, at least not for me, and so it couldn't be a more complex challenge. And even reading, going back to the question you asked, Mike, about reading all the attacks on deconstruction and on the academy in general, but particularly on deconstruction, in a book like David Lehman's book on de Man, what's interesting to me is that the repeated dismissals and denunciations of deconstruction in the form of generalizations is accompanied by Lehman actually using a lot of deconstructive techniques in his reading. And so he doesn't tell you what the techniques are, he only describes them from the outside. He doesn't go through an analysis and say, This is how Derrida reads, this is how de Man reads. He just says, They end up saying there is nothing outside the text and this is manifestly stupid. Then he will go and reread some pronouncements where he will say, This is internally self-contradictory, which is a gesture that is thoroughly deconstructive. And so, it's as if he wants to appropriate for himself in silence everything that deconstruction really does and use it against this figure that he sets up by using only declarative sentences and opinions about those declarative sentences as the object that he wants to dismiss. And so his book is probably the most complex among the criticisms, because he is, in fact, pretty good at doing what he calls 'soft-core' deconstructive reading. He will say, This text that I have received from the executive provost of something-or-another says that we should abolish hierarchy, but then why does he have to sign his letter 'executive provost of such and such'? And how a text has it both ways is very interesting to Lehman, and in some ways the whole enterprise of turning deconstruction against itself is itself a deconstructive act. He begins by showing how thoroughly 'disseminated' the word 'deconstruction' has become. But a deconstructor can't respond by correcting inaccuracies or bringing the word back to its 'true' meaning without a role switch. But of course, deconstruction wouldn't be as interesting as it is if it hadn't – both in Derrida and in de Man – acknowledged the inescapability of the desire to correct, to get it right, to tell the truth. So there too, it's hard to say what's the inside and what's the outside.

PAYNE Your essays display a great range of interest, and you seem to intersect with some of the most important features of the theoretical landscape: deconstruction, feminism, psychoanalysis, anti-racialism. Are all these interests compelling for you?

JOHNSON They are all intertwined.

PAYNE What about Marxism? This is one aspect of the current theoretical landscape that you don't give much space to in your work.

JOHNSON No, it's true. When I read Marx, I am filled with admiration. The clarity with which he analyzes economic structures, historical structures, the wonderful way he writes, the figures and allusions, the analytical gestures and procedures and so forth, I find utterly compelling. How to translate the insights of Marx and the procedures of Marx into literary criticism has certainly been worked out by a lot of more recent writers who . . . I guess I feel that I would need a different kind of training to do a Marxist analysis well and that there are certainly a lot of connections that have been made by Michael Ryan, Gayatri Spivak, Fred Jameson, and others about methods of analysis or kinds of questions that are central to both deconstruction and Marxism. In some ways you could say both that they are commentaries on Hegel and that they really do go in different directions, although procedurally there are a lot of similarities. I don't feel able to set up the grounds for a Marxist analysis; that is, it requires a certain kind of historical research and a sense of the overall historical narrative that I'm not yet well enough versed in.

SCHWEIZER Has the value of Marxist theory diminished after the historical events of the last two years?

JOHNSON I don't think the value of Marx has diminished as somebody who really made a difference in intellectual and political history, but I think there has always been a very loose connection between Marxist criticism and the structures of government in the Soviet Union and other places. I don't think Marxist criticism has been dependent on the existence of Communist systems of government; but the collapse of the Communist structure in the Soviet Union raises questions for Marxism that are necessary for Marxism to address, and I think it should. Obviously the fact that a government in practice didn't sustain itself or sustain the promises it made for itself doesn't at all mean that there wasn't wisdom in the theories that set it up. This may be a practical problem; this may be a problem about a system which would work if you could find a way of controlling it other than through an authoritarian apparatus. I mean, maybe that's the hard part. Who or what would insure that the system remained equitable?

SCHWEIZER I have another question that should, perhaps, have gone into the moment we spent some time ago when we talked about deconstruction. Could you explain that mysterious passage in one of your essays where you claim that what deconstruction shows is that there is something else involved that puts into question the separability of binary oppositions? Freud's example of such a something else, you mentioned there, is the death instinct, and my question is, Has deconstruction something similar to the death instinct to offer as an alternative logic to binary opposition?

JOHNSON   I think, yes, if it means that binary oppositions never really divide up the whole field, that there would always be a kind of unthought remainder that would be functioning nevertheless, even though it wasn't recognized. But I think it may *be* the death instinct also, in the sense that there is a formal overdetermination that is, in Freud's case, going to produce repetition or, in deconstruction's case, may inhere in linguistic structures that don't correspond to anything else.

PAYNE   You seem to value difficulty in what you write about the texts of Mallarmé and Lacan. You obviously have a great appetite for difficulty. Where does that come from? On what does valuing difficulty rest?

JOHNSON   It's not as if I think life is simple, so I retreat into literature so as to find the difficulty that I crave! I think, on the contrary, that life is extremely complex, and a literature that tries to work on what the nature of that complexity is interests me as a way of thinking about the difficulty life presents. So much of the indoctrination we get in the socialization process implies that everything should be simple. We should just love each other; men should just take care of the children half the time; that would be simple. What is it that resists those simple solutions that we all say we believe in? That's what I'm interested in, that kind of persistence of resistances to the simplicity that our ideology bombards us with as that which we fall short of through seemingly accidental fault.

PAYNE   Could difficulty be deconstruction's death instinct?

JOHNSON   It could be.

PAYNE   I ask that because in *Beyond the Pleasure Principle*, where Freud is going back and revising what psychoanalytic theory was until about 1925, it looks as though there may be a moment of abandonment of what it was that hinges on what the word 'beyond' means. Is pleasure being abandoned, or is it being deepened and enriched? And this leads me to the question, or another way of asking the question I asked before concerning the relation between difficulty and pleasure: Is there an indulgent intellectual pleasure in the pursuit of difficulty?

JOHNSON   Yes. It's a sort of make it last.

SCHWEIZER   One of the things that one finds out with advancing age is that pleasure is very serious.

PAYNE   Serious but not somber.

SCHWEIZER   That's right (*laughing*). It is one of the few indisputable things like pain or suffering that provides you with an epistemology.

JOHNSON   You mean that, no matter how hard you try, you can't avoid pleasure?

SCHWEIZER   I think it's something indisputable in the sense that it is an experience that is impossible not to have on some level of existence.

PAYNE One accusation against deconstruction is that people who practice it simply keep producing the same kind of interpretation for every text. This is perhaps pushing an analogy too far, but one aspect of the death instinct in the treatise of Freud relates to the compulsion to repeat. One repeats over and over again, not just in clinical sessions, but in one's life, not those things which are pleasurable, but one keeps making the same mistakes again and again and again. When deconstruction is true to itself, or when deconstructive critical practices are true to deconstructive processes in texts, is not the true difficulty an insistence that one must find the new?

JOHNSON Ah, so many thoughts occurred to me while you were talking. Now they are all gone. I think that it's like saying that from the outside someone's behavior looks like repetition, but from the inside it feels like life, or it feels like pleasure. Someone who repeatedly drinks too much or marries and divorces or buys a car and sells it for less than he paid for it. Whatever it is where you would say, This person seems to be living an absurd and repetitive life, always falling into the same mistake. But from the inside, the way the choices keep presenting themselves are what make the person feel that they are alive. And so, any kind of criticism that you're not involved in looks more repetitive from the outside than it feels from the inside. Not that you can't say there are some similarities and predictabilities. Take a hundred essays and you would certainly find similarities, but I think that people say the same thing about Marxist criticism or about feminist criticism or about New Criticism or about religious criticism or whatever, that, in fact, the repetition comes in the way an argument concludes. Therefore, that is not of interest. What is of interest is the possibility of there being an encounter somewhere along the way of the analysis with the unexpected or the overturning of presuppositions of the argument itself. It may look as if these are not overturning the expected, but I think the whole pleasure of analysis is when you say, Wow, the text has made me see something that I really didn't see the first time, or, This really gives me a new way of thinking about something. In a lot of essays you can sort of feel as if you get, or at least the author got, that feeling while pursuing the analysis. Pushing the text until it tells you something you didn't already know is probably what all good criticism does and I don't mean just the text but the whole inquiry – it could be the historical context. Therefore, it seems to me you could find good examples and bad examples of any critical school.

SCHWEIZER In *A World of Difference* you promise progress, and then think back and say, Maybe I didn't make so much progress. Were you trying to say just this, in so many words, in that introduction, that you were more engaged by the way in which you were surprised in the course of the individual essays than that these essays would make a certain progression towards . . .

JOHNSON Or that it occurred to me that my earlier work was more about life than I thought it was, or that I was thinking through things about life that I didn't realize I was thinking through. I thought that if I could now turn to those or, perhaps, just another displacement of those, I could say something more direct about life. But sometimes making a search more explicit makes it less insightful. Sometimes thinking you know what you are talking about diminishes the insight you might have reached by not knowing. I think sometimes displacement helps, so that's another way in which I would question the achievement of progress.

SCHWEIZER The question about a title might be a good question to close with. We were wondering whether, in the title *The Wake of Deconstruction* for the Bucknell lectures, there was some sort of ambiguity involved. We were not quite sure when you came here whether we were attending a funeral or whether we were celebrating the effects and influence of deconstruction. Perhaps on some level there is indeed some ambivalence about deconstruction. Your announcement of a progress in your book seems to point to a desire perhaps to see something beyond the surprises in the essays. It's an apocalyptic title in any case, isn't it?

JOHNSON In a sense. But I also think that this ambiguity of whether there is progress, of whether there is an identifiable lineage or genealogy flowing from deconstruction, whether deconstruction is awake or asleep and whether it's dead or alive and whether it ever was alive – that all those questions have in part to do with what can be called the negativity of deconstruction, by which I mean not that it has a bad attitude but that it is really in many ways a *response* to propositional thinking, or positivistic thinking, that it depends on the existence of other voices in order to do its work. And so it can't, in a way, stand alone; and if being alive is being, in some sense, autonomous (which is, I think, an erroneous assumption), then it has to have been, in some ways, always already dead. It always was contradictory to its stance for it to seem to dominate intellectual life. It really couldn't do that without losing its lack of ground. I think that the fact that it did have a sort of dominant role was paradoxical, and that part of the resistance to that dominant position in literary studies is a correct perception that deconstruction is not at its best in a dominant position. And maybe that's true of other analytical projects as well. Just as Marx in the *Eighteenth Brumaire* first gave a very clear and convincing analysis, even if it could be criticized on historical grounds I don't know; but the sense one has that he has revealed hidden connections and explained paradoxes in the way that people voted in 1848 is convincing, but that the minute he starts moving from the past to the future and making prophecies, he starts writing fiction. He says, Since I predicted that Napoleon's statue would fall, and it has, you should believe what I say about the future. And he predicts a whole future where there will be no such separation between what you would expect from economic structures and what you get from voting behavior. He bases his prophetic authority on an analytic authority derived from the explanation of discrepancies, but his prophecy will eliminate the discrepancies on which his analytical authority is based. This could be seen as an analogy to deconstruction, in that it needs those discrepancies it analyzes in order for its analytical activity to arrive at an insight-producing stance. But if deconstruction is setting the terms for what is to be analyzed next, then it's collapsing the room it needs to breathe in.

Barbara Johnson: A Bibliography, 1973–1993

Compiled by Mary E. Schoonover

1973

1 'La Vérité tue: une lecture de *Conte*,' *Littérature* 11 (October), pp. 68–77.

1975

2 'Défigurations,' *Littérature* 18 (May), pp. 100–10.

1976

3 'Quelques conséquences de la différence anatomique des textes,' *Poétique* 28 (December), pp. 450–65.

1977

4 (trans.), 'Fors: The Anglish Words of Nicolas Abraham and Maria Torok,' by Jacques Derrida, *Georgia Review* 31, pp. 64–116.
5 'Poetry and Performative Language,' *Yale French Studies* 54, pp. 140–58.
6 'The Frame of Reference: Poe, Lacan, Derrida,' *Yale French Studies* 55/56, pp. 457–505; different version in

Psychoanalysis and the Question of the Text, ed. Geoffrey H. Hartman (Baltimore: Johns Hopkins University Press, 1978), pp. 149–71; reprinted in *The Purloined Poe*, ed. John Muller and William Richardson (Baltimore: Johns Hopkins University Press, 1988), pp. 213–51; reprinted in *Ukradeni Poe* (Ljubljana, 1990), pp. 84–123.

7   (trans.), 'Freud's Hand,' by Philippe Sollers, *Yale French Studies* 55/56, pp. 329–37.

1978

8   'Crise de Prose,' *Po&sie* 4 (Spring), pp. 92–106.
9   'The Critical Difference,' *diacritics* 8, no. 2, pp. 2–9; reprinted *Pamietnik Literaki* 77, no. 2 (1986), pp. 297–306.

1979

10   *Défigurations du langage poétique: la seconde révolution baudelairienne* (Paris: Flammarion), 213 pp.
11   'Melville's Fist: The Execution of Billy Budd,' *Studies in Romanticism* 18, no. 4, pp. 567–99.

1980

12   *The Critical Difference: Essays in the Contemporary Rhetoric of Reading* (Baltimore: Johns Hopkins University Press), 156 pp.
13   'Nothing Fails Like Success,' *SCE Reports* 8 (Fall), pp. 7–16; reprinted in French, German and English in *Parallax* 1 (1989), pp. 25–34.

1981

14   (trans., notes, and introduction), *Dissemination*, by Jacques Derrida (Chicago: University of Chicago Press).
15   'Le Dernier Homme,' in *Les Fins de l'homme: actes du colloque de Cérisy sur Derrida* (Paris: Galilée); trans. as

'The Last Man,' in *The Other Mary Shelley*, ed. Esther Schor, Audrey Fisch, and Anne Mellor (Oxford: Oxford University Press, 1993), pp. 258–66.

16 'Les Fleurs du mal armé,' *Michigan Romance Studies* 2, pp. 87–99; reprinted in *Discours et pouvoir*, ed. Ross Chambers (Ann Arbor: Department of Romance Languages, University of Michigan, 1982), pp. 87–99; trans. and extended in *Lyric Poetry: Beyond New Criticism*, ed. Patricia Parker and Chaviva Hosek (Ithaca, N.Y.: Cornell University Press, 1985), pp. 264–80.

1982

17 (ed.), *Yale French Studies* 63: 'The Pedagogical Imperative: Teaching as a Literary Genre.'
18 'My Monster/My Self,' *diacritics* 12, no. 2, pp. 2–10.
19 'Teaching Ignorance: l'école des femmes,' *Yale French Studies* 63, pp. 165–82.

1983

20 'Disfiguring Poetic Language,' in *The Prose Poem in France: Theory and Practice*, ed. Mary Ann Caws and Hermine Riffaterre (New York: Columbia University Press), pp. 79–97.
21 (trans.), 'Poetry without Verse,' by Tzvetan Todorov in *The Prose Poem in France: Theory and Practice*, ed. Mary Ann Caws and Hermine Riffaterre (New York: Columbia University Press), pp. 60–78.

1984

22 'Gender Theory and the Yale School,' *Genre* 17, nos 1/2, pp. 101–12; reprinted in *Rhetoric and Form: Deconstruction at Yale*, ed. Robert Con Davis and Ronald Schleiffer (Norman: University of Oklahoma Press, 1985),

pp. 75–97; reprinted in *Speaking of Gender*, ed. Elaine Showalter (New York: Routledge, 1989), pp. 45–55.

23   'Mallarmé as Mother,' *Denver Quarterly* 18, no. 4, pp. 77–83.

24   'Metaphor, Metonymy and Voice in Zora Neale Hurston's *Their Eyes Were Watching God*,' in *Black Literature and Literary Theory*, ed. Henry Louis Gates, jr. (New York: Methuen), pp. 205–19; reprinted in *Textual Analysis: Some Readers Reading*, ed. Mary Ann Caws (New York: Modern Language Association of America, 1986), pp. 232–44.

25   'Rigorous Unreliability,' *Critical Inquiry* 11, no. 2, pp. 278–85; reprinted in *Yale French Studies* 69, pp. 73–80.

26   (panelist), 'Symposium: Marxism and Deconstruction,' *Genre* 17, nos 1/2, pp. 75–97.

1985

27   'In Memoriam: Paul de Man,' *Yale French Studies* 69, pp. 9–10.

28   'Taking Fidelity Philosophically,' in *Difference in Translation*, ed. Joseph Graham (Ithaca, N.Y.: Cornell University Press), pp. 142–8.

29   'Teaching Deconstructively,' in *Writing and Reading Differently: Deconstruction and the Teaching of Composition and Literature*, ed. G. Douglas Atkins and Michael L. Johnson (Lawrence: University Press of Kansas), pp. 140–8.

30   'Thresholds of Difference: Structures of Address in Zora Neale Hurston,' *Critical Inquiry* 12, no. 1, pp. 278–89; reprinted in *Race, Writing, and Difference*, ed. Henry Louis Gates, jr. (Chicago: University of Chicago Press, 1986), pp. 317–28.

1986

31   'Apostrophe, Animation, and Abortion,' *diacritics* 16, no. 1, pp. 29–47.

1987

32 *A World of Difference* (Baltimore: Johns Hopkins University Press), 225 pp.
33 (In collaboration with Marjorie Garber), 'Secret Sharing: Reading Conrad Psychoanalytically,' *College English* 49, no. 6, pp. 628–40.
34 Interview in *Criticism in Society*, by Imre Saluzinsky (New York: Methuen), pp. 151–75.

1988

35 'Deconstruction, Feminism, and Pedagogy,' in *Teaching Literature: What is Needed Now*, ed. James Engell and David Perkins (Cambridge, Mass.: Harvard University Press), pp. 67–72.
36 'Relevance of Theory/Theory of Relevance: Response to Michael Riffaterre,' *Yale Journal of Criticism* 1, no. 2, pp. 163–78.
37 'The Re(a)d and the Black: Richard Wright's Blueprint,' in *Modern Critical Interpretations of Richard Wright's Native Son*, ed. Harold Bloom (New York: Chelsea House), pp. 115–23; reprinted in *Reading Black, Reading Feminist*, ed. Henry Louis Gates, jr. (New York: Meridian, 1990), pp. 145–54.

1989

38 'Is Male to Female as Ground is to Figure?,' in *Feminism and Psychoanalysis*, ed. Richard Feldstein and Judith Roof (Ithaca, N.Y.: Cornell University Press), pp. 255–68.
39 Three entries in *A New History of French Literature*, ed. Denis Hollier (Cambridge, Mass.: Harvard University Press): 'The Lady in the Lake,' pp. 627–31; 'The Dream of Stone,' pp. 743–7; 'June: The Liberation of Verse,' pp. 798–800.
40 'Response to Henry Louis Gates, Jr.,' in *Afro-American Literary Study in the 1990s*, ed. Houston A. Baker, jr., and

Patricia Redmond (Chicago: University of Chicago Press), pp. 39–43.

41 'Interview with Hulk Hogan,' *Blast Unlimited* no. 1, pp. 8–11, 30–1.

1990

42 (ed., in collaboration with Jonathan Arac), *Consequences of Theory*, (Baltimore: Johns Hopkins University Press).

43 'Euphemism, Understatement, and the Passive Voice: A Genealogy of Afro-American Poetry,' in *Reading Black, Reading Feminist*, ed. Henry Louis Gates, jr. (New York: Meridian), pp. 204–11.

44 'A Note on the Wartime Writings of Paul de Man,' in *Literary Theory Today*, ed. Peter Collier and Helga Ryan (Ithaca, N.Y.: Cornell University Press), pp. 13–26.

45 'Gender and Poetry: Charles Baudelaire and Marceline Desbordes-Valmore,' in *Displacements: Women, Tradition, Literatures in French*, ed. Joan de Jean and Nancy K. Miller (Baltimore: Johns Hopkins University Press), pp. 163–81.

46 'Philology: What is at Stake?,' *Comparative Literature Studies* 27, no. 1, pp. 26–30; reprinted in *On Philology*, ed. Jan Ziolkowski (University Park: Penn State University Press, 1990), pp. 26–30.

47 'Poison or Remedy? Paul de Man as Pharmakon,' *Colloquium Helveticum* 11/12, pp. 7–20.

48 'Writing,' in *Critical Terms for Literary Study*, ed. Frank Lentricchia and Thomas McLaughlin (Chicago: University of Chicago Press), pp. 39–49.

1992

49 'Discard or Masterpiece? Mallarmé's *Le Livre*,' in *The Marks in the Fields*, ed. Rodney G. Dennis and Elizabeth Falsey (Cambridge, Mass.: Harvard University Press), pp. 145–50.

50 'The Postmodern in Feminism: A Response to Mary Joe Frug,' *Harvard Law Review* 105, no. 5, pp. 1076–83.

51 'The Quicksands of the Self: Nella Larsen and Heinz Kohut,' in *Telling Facts: History and Narration in Psychoanalysis*, ed. Joseph H. Smith and Humphrey Morris (Baltimore: Johns Hopkins University Press), pp. 184–99.

1993

52 (ed.), *Freedom and Interpretation: Oxford Amnesty Lectures 1992* (New York: Basic Books).

53 ' "Aesthetic" and "Rapport" in Toni Morrison's *Sula*', in *Textual Practice* no. 2, pp. 165–72.

54 'Lesbian Spectacles: Reading *Sula, Passing, Thelma and Louise*, and *The Accused*,' in *Media Spectacles*, ed. Marjorie Garber, Jann Matlock, and Rebecca Walkowitz (New York: Routledge), pp. 160–116.

55 'Moses and Intertextuality: Sigmund Freud, Zora Neale Hurston, and the Bible,' in *Intertextuality and Civilization in the Americas*, ed. J. Jefferson Humphries (Baton Rouge: Louisiana State University Press, forthcoming).

56 'The Alchemy of Style and Law,' in *The Rhetoric of Law*, ed. Austin Sarat (Ann Arbor: University of Michigan Press, forthcoming).

Index